W| LEPEN

D0305949

ock

CPC UCW
LLYFRGELL
LIBRARY
ABERYSTWYTH

4
104
E7

Escalation and Intervention

8080070950

CÍ 108 E7

Coleg Prifysgol Cymru
The University College of Wales
Aberystwyth

Acc. No. 8086070950

Class No. 𝒰 104 E7

About the Book and Editors

Since World War II, the international community has tried to insulate, limit, and resolve local conflicts. The generally poor success record has led some to conclude that multilateral organizations have failed in dealing with international conflicts, while others have argued that governments have not used these organizations effectively. Not enough thought, however, has been given to the contributions that can be made to conflict management and resolution through the use of diplomatic, political, military, and economic intervention by multilateral organizations, by unilateral action of national states, and by efforts of states acting in informal concert.

This book evaluates the means that have been used to influence the course of six recent disputes, considering the costs and benefits in each case. In a broader context, it examines the relationship of local conflict to international security and considers the dilemma of providing security to small states without compromising their independence. Finally, it assesses the extent to which local wars tend to escalate and threaten the global security system.

Arthur R. Day is a senior consultant to the United Nations Association of the USA and has served as deputy assistant secretary of state for Near Eastern and South Asian affairs. **Michael W. Doyle** is associate professor of political science at The Johns Hopkins University.

Published in cooperation
with the United Nations Association
of the United States of America

Escalation and Intervention

Multilateral Security
and Its Alternatives

edited by Arthur R. Day
and Michael W. Doyle

Westview Press • Boulder, Colorado

Mansell Publishing Limited • London, England

This volume is included in Westview's Special Studies in International Security

All rights reserved. No part of this publication may be reproduced or transmitted in any form or by any means, electronic or mechanical, including photocopy, recording, or any information storage and retrieval system, without permission in writing from Westview Press.

Copyright © 1986 by Westview Press, Inc.

Published in 1986 in the United States of America by Westview Press, Inc.; Frederick A. Praeger, Publisher; 5500 Central Avenue, Boulder, Colorado 80301

Published in 1986 in Great Britain by Mansell Publishing Limited, 6 All Saints Street, London N1 9RL

Library of Congress Cataloging-in-Publication Data
Escalation and intervention: multilateral security
    and its alternatives.
    (Westview special studies in international security)
    Contents: Conflict in Chad / I. William Zartman—
Civil conflict in Lebanon / Arthur Day—The Iran-Iraq
war / Barry Rubin—[etc.]
    1. Escalation (Military science)—Addresses, essays,
lectures.   2. Conflict management—Addresses, essays,
lectures.   3. Security, International—Addresses,
essays, lectures.   4. Military history, Modern—20th
century—Addresses, essays, lectures.   5. World
politics—1975–1985—Addresses, essays, lectures.
I. Day, Arthur R.   II. Doyle, Michael W.   III. Series.
U104.E83 1986   327.1′6   86-4020
ISBN 0-8133-7200-3

British Library Cataloguing in Publication Data
Escalation and intervention: multilateral security and its alternatives.
    1. Arms control.
    I. Day, Arthur R.   II. Doyle, Michael W.
327.1′74   JX1974
ISBN 0-7201-1847-6

Composition for this book was provided by the editors.
This book was produced without formal editing by the publishers.

Printed and bound in the United States of America

The paper used in this publication meets the requirements of the American National Standard for Permanence of Paper for Printed Library Materials Z39.48-1984.

6   5   4   3   2   1

Contents

Preface

This book is the product of a study undertaken in 1984–85 by the Multilateral Project of the United Nations Association of the USA. The study was intended to serve two of the principal purposes of the Project: to promote the development of better means to control and to resolve local conflicts and to spur a more realistic public debate about the efficacy of multilateral means, relative to other methods, to deal with conflict.

The study developed through a series of stages designed to bring academic experts together with professionals in the foreign policy field. After the authors had been chosen for the chapters on individual conflicts, meetings were held in which they discussed with academic experts from other disciplines, with UN officials, and with former US government officials the issues the study was intended to cover. When the chapters on the six conflicts were completed, in May 1985, a larger conference was held, of essentially the same groups of participants, in association with the Stanley Foundation of Muscatine, Iowa, to assess the conclusions that could be drawn from the cases studied. The Conclusions section is much indebted to the work of this conference.

The United Nations Association, and the book's editors in particular, deeply appreciate the interest, encouragement, and cooperation of the authors who participated in writing the book. Professor Zartman was especially helpful with advice and in reviewing the Conclusions section. Others who took part at various stages of the study and assisted in bringing it to a fruitful outcome included Professor John Gerard Ruggie of Columbia University, who chaired the May 1985 conference and reviewed the Conclusions section; James Sutterlin, George Sherry (now retired), and S. Iqbal Riza of the UN Secretariat; Professor John Murphy of Villanova University; former US Ambassador James F. Leonard, Chairman of the Board of the Committee for National Security; and former US Ambassador Donald Easum, President of the African-American Institute. All participated in one or more of the meetings with the study's authors. UN Under Secretaries General Brian Urquhart (now retired) and Diego Cordovez were generous with information and encouragement. Susan Koehrsen and Jeffrey Martin of the Stanley Foundation were expert and helpful in connection with the May 1985 conference.

Many United Nations Association staff members provided invaluable support and assistance. Frederic Eckhard (now in the UN Secretariat) headed the Multilateral Project during the period of the study. Ann Florini gave useful advice while conducting a successful project among UNA chapters and affiliated organizations on much the same subject. Cheryl Robinson struggled successfully over the months putting drafts of the book into the word processor and Susan Woolfson did a superlative job of coding for publication, while Constance Carpenter put the coded text into final shape on the disks. Linda Horkitz helped greatly to bring readability and consistency to the text.

The study was funded largely through grants to UNA's Multilateral Project by the James S. McDonnell Foundation and the Armand Hammer Foundation, as well as by generous individual contributions. The MacArthur Foundation is funding a UNA project that will emphasize public involvement in the consideration of conflict management and resolution; this book will be one of the source materials employed by the project.

*   *   *

The United Nations Association of the USA is a national organization that conducts programs of research, study, and information to increase public knowledge of global issues and the relationship of these issues to the United Nations system; to encourage, where appropriate, multilateral approaches in dealing with these issues; to build public support for constructive US policies on matters of global concern; and to enhance the effectiveness of the United Nations and other multilateral institutions.

UNA-USA carries out its programs through a network of national and community organizations and leaders. This network comprises 175 chapters and divisions throughout the country and 130 affiliated national organizations. Participants in UNA's programs come from business, labor, and academia; many have held senior positions in the US government and the United Nations.

UNA-USA is a private, nonprofit, nonpartisan organization.

Arthur R. Day
Michael W. Doyle

Introduction

Michael W. Doyle

As a provider of international security, the United Nations has fallen on hard times. This is hardly a new or startling development. Indeed, United Nations Secretary General Javier Pérez de Cuéllar himself best described the problem when in 1982 he declared that the United Nations "often finds itself unable to take decisive action to resolve conflicts and its resolutions are increasingly defied or ignored by those who feel themselves strong enough to do so."[1] Yet like the feisty but bedridden octogenarian whose reply to the question "How's life?" was "Compared to what?", scholars and statesmen interested in international security need to evaluate multilateral international organizations such as the United Nations, the Organization of American States (OAS), and the Organization of African Unity (OAU) in light of the performance of their leading alternatives.

In order to understand how various forms of diplomacy can best complement each other, we have asked how well unilateral interventions, bilateral diplomacy, and ad hoc multinational forces have done in securing the interests of the states that used them. What have they done to promote international order? These questions seem to us to have been missing in much of the debate concerning the failings of international organizations. We have therefore undertaken this study of recent important cases of negotiation and intervention in third world conflicts. We have assessed the successes and failures of multilateral diplomacy and intervention. We have tried to assess the costs and benefits of the use of alternatives to multilateral means. And in the many instances where multilateral means were neglected, we have tried to consider whether they might have been used, especially in combination with non-multilateral means, throughout a dispute or at different stages, and with what consequences.

The pursuit of alternatives to multilateral security has been stimulated in part by the longstanding weaknesses of the United Nations and the regional organizations as providers of international security.[2] A recent assessment by a leading scholar in the field concludes that developments since 1970 have constituted an even further decline of the reliability of multilateral international security.[3] Ernst Haas has noted that the record of the United Nations and the Organization of American States in abating, isolating, and settling disputes as well as in stopping hostilities has worsened. Other organizations such as the Arab League or the Organization of African Unity have not compensated for the decline of the UN and the OAS. International secretariats and the major powers no longer exercise the leadership they once did. And rhetorical posturing rather than mediation and peacekeeping have increasingly characterized multilateral approaches to conflicts, as we have seen in Timor, Lebanon, the Arab-Israeli wars, Cambodia, the Falkland Islands, Namibia, Angola, South Africa, and the Iran-Iraq war.[4]

In recent discussions of multilateral security, few dispute the existence of a problem. But in the literature on international organization, many clash over its causes and potential cures. Some find sources of discord in the structure of the postwar international distribution of power, leading to neglect of the institutions of multilateral security. Others see managerial problems that can be overcome by technical fixes and greater determination ("political will") on the part of the members. And still others see constitutional flaws in the United Nations as an institution that have made it "outdated" before its time.

The structural critique is probably the most widely shared. Some commentators and the smaller states in particular have seen multilateral security as a noble effort to preserve "succeeding generations from the scourge of war," as the UN Charter puts it, "to unite our strength to maintain international peace," and "to ensure, by the acceptance of principles and the institution of methods, that armed force shall not be used, save in the common interest." According to tradition, a workable system that makes the security of all into a collective responsibility requires commitment on the part of states to protect all states ("peace is indivisible") and a distribution of power among states such that no state is capable of effectively resisting the collective enforcement of peace.[5]

The postwar international system, however, has been characterized by three international revolutions that have made indivisibility and collective enforcement very problematic. First, beginning in 1945, nuclear weapons entered the arsenals of the major powers. In the 1950's and 1960's, these weapons transformed the security capabilities and strategies of the major powers from defense to deterrence. Second, by the end of the 1940's, US-Soviet bipolarity had clearly replaced the multipolarity characteristic of the traditional European diplomatic arena. And third, the movement for self-determination, starting with the independence of India in 1947 and rapidly spreading in the 1950's and 1960's to the rest of Asia, the Middle East, Africa, and the Caribbean, discredited the political foundations of the colonial empires, leading to the independence of scores of new states.

Each of these postwar "revolutions" undermined the operation of collective international security. Bipolarity and nuclear weapons worked against indivisibility and effective collective enforcement. All wars are simply not the same when some can involve nuclear states. Punishing or even attempting to stop a nuclear state can be irrational and can even put at risk the survival of states prepared to join the collective force. But bipolarity, even without the invention of nuclear weapons, would have discredited the guarantee against aggression that collective security has traditionally promised, for no coalition enforcing collective security could have been overwhelming unless it included both super-powers.[6]

The arrival of more than a hundred new states in a short space of time had an equally revolutionary effect on international security. It imposed a severe burden on all forms of international security, including even peacekeeping and international mediation. These states have not, for the most part, had the time to develop secure political authority domestically. Most of them inherited arbitrary colonial boundaries incorporating disparate racial, ethnic, and religious communities. In many cases, colonial policy encouraged an extensive development of the local colonial capital and the growth of a bureaucracy that served it, without having a similar impact on the surrounding countryside. Few have developed economies capable of sustaining extensive sources of communication, economic integration, or state taxation. They thus are subject to large, particularistic demands from the separate communities that make up the state, but they have small material resources with which to satisfy those demands. Frequently, according to students of the development process, government policy after independence has served to exacerbate, not to mitigate, these disruptive tendencies.

Consequently, almost all these newly independent states suffer from what might be called a double security dilemma. Whereas most governments find their security endangered from without, these governments face equally serious threats from within. "Many third world leaders," as Richard H. Ullman noted in a study of third world militarization, "face a problem that the leaders of Western great powers, if not those of the Soviet Union, do not: the fact that they themselves lack legitimacy in the eyes of important groups within their own societies. Unable to rule by consent, they feel constrained to rule by force of arms."[7] There are significant exceptions to this generalization. As Ullman argued, states such as Saudi Arabia appear to retain traditional legitimacy; the Costa Ricas of the third world appear to have managed the transition to popular legitimacy. But, the structuralists note, many third world governments are caught in an authoritarian dilemma wherein ruling by force doubles a government's potential enemies. This system of governing creates domestic opponents who are prone to support subversion, calling themselves "national liberators" and "freedom fighters" (which they may indeed be). It makes capitalist authoritarian states especially vulnerable to destabilization exported by Communists or third world nationalists; it makes socialist authoritarian states the nearly automatic enemies of liberal democratic states, which tend to have a strong distaste for authoritarian regimes, particularly those of the left.[8] And just as increasing a state's armaments in order to become more secure from foreign enemies may be counterproductive (as foreign states respond in kind), so increasing governmental repression in order to control domestic dissidents may only generate further dissidence.

The structuralist interpretation tells us that the United Nations system of collective international security has suffered from a triple burden. Bipolarity and nuclear weapons work against the indivisibility of peace and the predominance of collective enforcement that the collective-security tradition posits as necessary. At the same time, third world instability and revolutionary wars raise the demand for external sources of security, while they erode the traditional distinctions between civil and international war that made identifying the aggressor feasible. Under these circumstances, the UN and regional "failures" in maintaining collective international security can hardly be seen as surprising.

Nonetheless, the second interpretation stresses not the structural sources of failure but correctable mistakes and missing techniques. Thus, according to some, all states should accept the compulsory jurisdiction of the International Court of Justice; others propose that the Security Council should have a better communications network (satellites, perhaps). To others, the secretary general deserves a wider competence or should be limited to a single but longer term of office, increasing his independence by freeing him from the constraint of running for office. A problem with compulsory jurisdiction is illustrated by the current approach of the United States to the case brought by Nicaragua to the International Court. The US commitment to the jurisdiction of the court apparently has little force even for a small case such as this one. The value of an independent secretary general can already be seen in the candid approach taken to his responsibilities by Pérez de Cuéllar, who has announced an intention to hold his office for only one term. But the administrative and technical fixes are not solutions to the structural dilemmas discussed above, and few of their serious advocates regard them as such. Instead, the largest mistake, as seen from this viewpoint, is the failure of states to make adequate use of the collective institutions that the United Nations and the regional organizations provide.

Agreeing or disagreeing with this judgment, however, requires first assessing an objection that sees the problem of international security not in the international system but in the United Nations itself as a flawed institution. This third interpretation of the failures of the United Nations and the regional institutions holds much more sway. It says that not only is the structural burden of the postwar international system heavy but that the UN institution is flawed: outdated, it is said, before its time and designed for a world that never happened. This view has much to be said for it.[9] The actual shape the postwar system took was not anticipated during World War II, when Stalin, Roosevelt, and Churchill appeared to anticipate a continuation of an international system that would be multipolar, colonial, and conventionally armed. But this view misses an important degree of flexibility built into the UN's institutional framework.

While it is true that Article 43 (which commits members to specify the forces they would contribute) and Article 47 (which designates a Military Staff Committee to be a UN general staff for enforcement) were never implemented as planned, forces for the Korean operation were easily acquired on an ad hoc basis (sixteen members participated but 89 percent of the non-Korean forces were US forces). Article 27 (the veto power of the permanent members of the Security Council) made enforcement actions directed against the major powers or the clients they wished to protect impossible; this limitation, however, did not preclude actions against threats to the peace in which the permanent members perceived a common interest in preserving international security.[10] Examples of these actions include the Indo-Pakistani war of 1965 and the 1973 Arab-Israeli war in which the Security Council convincingly demanded a halt to hostilities. More significantly, we should recall that the Charter commitment to maintaining international peace and security was not designed to operate against the interests of the permanent members. Indeed, that is exactly what the veto power was intended to prevent. In the familiar analogy, the veto served as the fuse—a deliberately contrived weak point—installed to prevent an overload of collective commitments that would endanger the individual security of the members.[11] (The passage of the "Uniting for Peace" resolution of 1950, which attempted to circumvent the Security Council's veto provision with General Assembly majorities, was the equivalent of replacing a fuse with a penny.)

By those arguments, the Charter was designed to accommodate the major powers and can thus incorporate bipolarity and nuclear weapons. But can it operate when the third world's post-colonial instability produces exceptional strategic vulnerability and where the erosion of distinctions between civil and international war makes the identification of aggressors problematical? Article 10 of the League of Nations Covenant pledged its members "to respect and preserve as against external aggression the territorial integrity and existing political boundaries of all." International coercion and subversion, destroying political independence without external attack, fell outside its protection; so, too, did the most horrendous instances of purely domestic oppression, which served to undermine international society in the 1930's.

The Charter does not similarly handicap the United Nations. Article 1, paragraph 1, defines the purposes of the United Nations as not merely to curb aggression but to "maintain international peace and security," which includes not only removing "threats to the peace" but also taking measures for the "prevention" of threats and settling "situations which might lead to a breach of the peace." The preamble and the "Purposes and Principles" (Article 1:3) also cover encouraging a respect for fundamental human rights and promoting international cooperation of an "economic, social, cultural or humanitarian character." Although states are protected from interference concerning matters "essentially" (Article 2:7) within their domestic jurisdiction, even this exclusion is explicitly overridden for matters that may involve enforcement measures for international peace and security.[12]

The Security Council, in effect, was empowered to decide what is and what is not within the domestic jurisdiction of states. States retained an individual and collective right to protect themselves from "armed attack," but only the Council and "regional arrangements" (Article 52) that were consistent with the "Purposes and Principles" of the Charter (including, for example, sovereign equality) possessed the wider right and obligation to preserve international peace and security.

Endowing the United Nations with this capacity does not appear to have been accidental. Given the history of subversion in the 1930's and the collapse of international security more generally during that period, it would have been surprising if statesmen had not attempted to provide some security against repetition. In fact, this history seems to have been very much in the mind of the negotiators of the UN Charter. In 1945, in reporting on the negotiations in San Francisco, US Secretary of State Edward R. Stettinius noted that drawing up the clause for international security was particularly challenging: "The problem was especially complicated by the progress in modern techniques of warfare and the development of novel methods of propaganda and provocation."[13]

Nor has the United Nations been hesitant in seeking out perceived root causes of international insecurity. The Security Council has taken direct action against matters that by a traditional reading of international law would be within the domestic jurisdiction of the state in question. In 1961 the Council authorized action including force to prevent a civil war in the Congo (resolution 161) and finally authorized the UN force to remove the Tshombe regime from Katanga Province.[14] In 1966 Council resolution 221 imposed an embargo on and authorized Britain to intervene forcibly against Rhodesia in order to restore law and order and to guarantee fundamental human rights for the black majority after Rhodesia's unilateral declaration of independence in 1965. Various denunciations of and embargoes against South Africa's apartheid system by the General Assembly and the Security Council are of course also part of this commitment to preserve the wider foundations of collective security.[15]

If these arguments are correct, the United Nations does not suffer from specifically institutional, or constitutional, paralysis. It is fully capable of authorizing and conducting whatever measures its members might desire that promote the Charter's "Purposes and Principles" and that accord with its own voting procedures. And these procedures are not particularly limiting. Indeed, should the permanent members, by some extremely unlikely turn of events, ever reach a condominium, there is little in the UN Charter that would constitutionally prevent the world body from being employed to enforce a global imperium over the smaller states.

Instead, of course, the division among the permanent members (particularly, the cold war between the United States and the Soviet Union) has not only protected the independence of the small states, but it has also helped make the United Nations ineffective in maintaining international peace and security. The organization's security role has been correspondingly reduced to the limited, albeit valuable, role of diplomatic mediation and of providing accredited peacekeeping forces for disputes where both parties agree to introduce them.

Our own approach to the problems of international collective security falls in between these three interpretations. We start with a recognition of the problems that the current international structure poses for collective measures to promote international security. Given the always-present threat of nuclear war between the superpowers, we consider the prospects of escalation to nuclear warfare. We are also concerned about the mounting toll in lives, postponed civil governance, and delayed economic development that have followed from endemic violence in the third world.

We are equally unpersuaded by the two views of the UN's putative role in curbing international violence. We doubt that the organization could be transformed by a technical fix and do not think that it should be condemned to irrelevance by its Charter. We by and large accept the view that the United Nations is extremely limited in what it can undertake in practice. But we suspect that the calculation on the part of member states of what the United Nations and the regional organizations can appropriately handle has been skewed by a failure to compare multilateral costs and benefits to their non-multilateral alternatives. Our case studies thus have been constructed to explore multilateral and non-multilateral means in specific contexts and particularly to discuss when those means could best be combined.

We have sought to analyze hard disputes of the sort that would have challenged any form of diplomacy. Our choices were also motivated by a desire to have a wide range of cases involving both of the superpowers, some of the middle powers, and some of the states of the third world remote from superpower confrontation.

We begin with civil wars in Chad and Lebanon that escalated to the stage where they came to involve the active participation of outside powers. And we explore whether this escalation has been conducive to the settlement or management of these wars. We then consider two cases of international war in the third world—the Iran-Iraq war and the conflict in the Horn of Africa—and examine the successes and failures of multilateral and non-multilateral efforts. Here we focus on what sort of attention—from diplomatic to economic to humanitarian— has helped or might still help settle or isolate these disputes. Our last pair of cases involves an examination of two domestic conflicts in small and remote countries that rapidly escalated to the stage of superpower intervention but that stopped short of becoming superpower confrontations. We consider the outcomes in Afghanistan and Grenada and try to determine whether multilateral means were to some degree responsible for the different development of the two conflicts and whether such methods still could help in the achievement of a secure independence for each of the two countries.

Notes

1. "Annual Report of the UN Secretary-General," quoted in *The New York Times*, September 7, 1982.

2. One of the early arguments for seeking out alternatives to the United Nations was by Robert E. Osgood, "Woodrow Wilson, Collective Security, and the Lessons of History," *Confluence* (Winter 1957), p. 354.

3. Ernst B. Haas, "Regime Decay: Conflict Management and International Organizations, 1945–1981," *International Organization* 37, 2 (Spring 1983).

4. Haas, pp. 189–190.

5. The necessary commitment to the indivisibility of peace ironically was most eloquently expressed by Emperor Haile Selassie in his address to the League of Nations during Mussolini's attack against Ethiopia, *League of Nations*

Official Journal, Records of the 16th Ordinary Session of the Assembly, Special Supplement 151, Text of Debates, Part II. For the objective conditions required by collective security see Inis Claude, *Power and International Relations* (New York: Random House, 1962).

6. See Claude, *Power and International Relations* for a systematic discussion of the effects of these two developments on collective security.

7. Richard H. Ullman, "Arresting the Militarization of the Third World," in Jagat S. Mehta, ed., *Third World Militarization* (Austin: The Lyndon B. Johnson School of Public Affairs, 1985), p. 214.

8. Although domestic strife within third world states tends to draw in foreign intervention, third world states are not simply easy prey for intervention as were, for example, the societies of the nineteenth-century periphery that became subject to colonial rule. Often a foreign intervention today will itself mobilize one or more resistance movements, as in Vietnam and Afghanistan. The contrast drawn is between the contemporary third world and the members of the traditional state system. For a discussion of the political circumstances of contemporary intervention see Hedley Bull, "Intervention in the Third World," in H. Bull, ed., *Intervention in World Politics* (Oxford: Clarendon Press, 1984).

9. There are of course many denunciations of the United Nations for being a fundamentally flawed (to some, "outdated") institution (and the number of denunciations has increased in recent years). But there are also thoughtful and sympathetic studies that arrive at similar conclusions. I have had the benefit of reading in draft one of the latter by Alan James, "The United Nations and the Maintenance of International Peace and Security: A Retrospective and Prospective View," intended for publication in a collection of articles by the United Nations Institute for Training and Research (UNITAR).

10. See the analysis by Jock A. Finlayson and Mark W. Zacher, "The United Nations and Collective Security: Retrospect and Prospect," in Toby Trister Gati, ed., *The US, the UN, and the Management of Global Change* (New York: UNA-USA/NYU Press, 1985), pp. 162–183.

11. Claude, *Swords Into Plowshares* (New York: Random House, 1971), p. 156.

12. A careful legal analysis of this question is given by Leo Gross in "Domestic Jurisdiction, Enforcement Measures and the Congo," in Leo Gross, ed., *Essays on International Law and Organization*, Vol. II (Dobbs Ferry, NY: Transnational Publishers, 1984), pp. 1173–1192.

13. Edward R. Stettinius, *Report to the President on the Results of the San Francisco Conference*, June 26, 1945, Dept. of State Publication 2349, Conference Series 71 (Washington: Govt. Printing Office, 1945), pp. 91–92.

14. For a discussion of the Congo case see Gross, above, and John F. Murphy, *The United Nations and the Control of Violence* (Totowa, NJ: Allanheld and Osmun, 1982), pp. 156–161, which finds that the UN action was too coercive to be a peacekeeping venture and too informal to be a Chapter 7 enforcement (although on the relation between Articles 42 and 43 see Gross, p. 1184). The complexities of the case are indicated by the fact that the United Nations intervened at the invitation of a central government whose existence was soon

in doubt and then put down a secession in the name of the self-defense of the peacekeeping force.

15. For discussions of a wide range of cases see Ernst Haas, Joseph Nye, and R.L. Butterworth, *Managing Interstate Conflict, 1945–74: Data with Synopses* (Pittsburgh: University Center of International Studies, 1976). For a commentary on South Africa, see p. 274.

PART ONE

Domestic Conflicts

I

Conflict in Chad

I. William Zartman

Three Rings of Conflict

The conflict in Chad runs in three concentric circles. It began as a domestic political conflict over the distribution of scarce resources among the various regional and ethnic groups of the country. As this conflict gradually proceeded to destroy political authority in the country and to create a political vacuum, neighboring African states began to take a more active role, opening a second ring of participants. In response to this widening conflict, non-African powers have been drawn in from time to time, giving the struggle a global aspect.

The result of the inner conflict has been the collapse of the Chadian state, challenging internal and external participants with the difficult task of reconstituting political authority. The result of the second ring of conflict has been the invasion of the country by its neighbor, Libya, and its occupation by a number of defensive forces seeking to provide law and order, including French troops and an Inter-African Force (IAF) sponsored by the Organization of African Unity (OAU). The result of the third ring has been sporadic interference by non-African powers, not only France but also the United States and the Soviet Union, at least as arms sources. As long as any party had a chance to opt out of an emerging reconciliation and to fight on to win, no conflict management was possible. However, by the end of 1984, the conflict appeared to have wound down to its original dimensions, and the makings of a stable outcome seemed to be emerging through the combined and appropriately timed efforts of external powers, African states, and Chadian leaders.

I. William Zartman is professor of international politics and African studies at the Johns Hopkins University School of Advanced International Studies. He is the author of numerous books and articles on Africa and on means of dealing with international conflict; his most recent book is *Ripe for Resolution* (New York: Oxford University Press, 1985).

Internal Conflict

The internal conflict in Chad has its roots in the history of the region, before a country called Chad ever existed. The region is the home of shifting kingdoms, slave raids and warfare, and unstable relations among groups characteristic of the Sahelian "shatter zone," where Arab populations from the north and east met a number of central African groups from the south and west.[1] Compounding this canvas of conflict is a warrior and raiding tradition in the sparsely populated north, covering the caravan routes between black and Arab Africa. Colonization in its turn added its sources of conflict by concentrating its effects on the productive and accessible area and on the more numerous and receptive population of the south. In 1960, independence came to a new state, Chad, ruled by southern politicians led by François (later Ngarta) Tombalbaye, but not yet constituting a nation. The subsequent history of the country has been one of successive attempts at state-building, each collapsing successively under its own failings.

Part of this collapse has been the work of the Chadians themselves, part the work of nature. The basic fact of life in Chad is poverty; the country has one of the smallest per capita incomes in the world ($120), which has been going down at an annual rate of 5 percent since 1970. It has no raw materials, despite some rumor of uranium in the extreme north, and cotton is almost its only export. Poverty does not only mean a primitive and precarious life for the Chadian people; it also means a political system with few resources out of which to reward followers, stimulate energies, create incentives, and solve problems. When the trough is small, groups fight hard for a turn at it and they fight for keeps.

During the first five years of independence, Tombalbaye consolidated his hold on the country, abolished all parties but his own Chadian People's Party (PPT) in 1962, elected a rubber-stamp parliament in 1964, and governed for the benefit of the south, ignoring the north. In 1965, he dismissed the French Army and replaced it with Chadian administrators in the north to collect new taxes and compulsory national loans. Revolt broke out in the north, and in 1966 the rebel forces joined together in a loosely organized grouping called the National Liberation Front of Chad (FroLiNaT). The revolt spread against continuing government policies of southern dominance and northern neglect and repression.

Return of French Troops

Beginning in late 1968, Tombalbaye launched a number of different strategies to defend his regime. French troops returned to northern

Chad, but the following year Tombalbaye agreed to accept a French Administrative Reform Mission (MRA) to reduce conflict instead of merely combating it. The MRA sought to install a more decentralized administration and to involve greater Moslem (northern) participation in the central government. Elections were held in 1969 and the government was reorganized. However, the arrival of Colonel Muammar el-Qaddafi in power in Libya the same year brought new support to the FroLiNaT, leading to an attempted coup in 1971 and a commando attack on Ndjamena, the capital, in 1972. Tombalbaye then turned to Libya to undercut its support for the rebels; in December 1972, he visited Qaddafi, receiving economic aid; and the following year he inaugurated a cultural revolution involving enforced traditional practices and name changes for places and people (including himself). Tombalbaye also secretly ceded the northern `Aouzou Strip of the country to Libya, which occupied and annexed it in 1973. Nevertheless, the rebellion continued as younger leaders replaced the original figures. The `Aouzou issue split the new FroLiNaT leadership; Hissen Habré, the original commander of the Armed Forces of the North (FAN), opposed the cession, but Goukouni Oueddei, who accepted the Libyan claims, ousted Habré in 1976 with Libyan help and reorganized part of the FroLiNaT as the People's Armed Forces (FAP). The French Army left in 1972 in the belief that order was restored, and for the following few years there was a lull in the civil conflict.

The cultural revolution alienated Tombalbaye's own southern followers and led to a military coup in 1975; Tombalbaye was killed. The new President, General Felix Malloum, dismissed the remaining French troops, but the rebellion continued. In 1977, the French Army returned to aid the Chadian Armed Forces (FAT) and, at the same time, to press again for reconciliation among the several parts of the country. In 1978, Habré was brought into a government of national union as Prime Minister, a basic charter was negotiated, the FAT and the FAN were combined into a national army, and a Defense and Security Council composed equally of Malloum's and Habré's followers replaced the Supreme Military Council as the national policy body. This dual partnership broke down in February 1979 under the pressure of personal rivalries, structural stalemate and imbalance, and unresolved local grievances. Habré turned against Malloum's forces and drove them out of the capital, moving the civil war to the southern part of the country.

Neighboring States

Faced with the collapse of government, the African neighbors of Chad moved into action. Between March and August 1979, four meetings were held in Nigeria attended by neighboring and other African states and representatives of the eleven factions of the FroLiNaT, who were party to the conflict.[2] The result was a Transitional Government of National Unity (GUNT) presided over by Goukouni with Malloum's lieutenant Abd-el-Kader Kamougue as Vice-President and Habré as Defense Minister. Within six months, the unity of the GUNT also collapsed into anarchy, and a succession of foreign forces made their attempts at restoring domestic order. Nigerian troops came to Ndjamena in March 1979 as peacekeeping forces as agreed at the first Nigerian meeting held in Kano, but the Chadian government soon asked them to leave because of policy differences and an attitude the Chadians found offensive. The French troops were phased out between late 1979 and May 1980, as the Chadians tried to go it alone without the continued presence of the former colonizer. An Inter-African Force of troops from Guinea, Benin, and the Congo, agreed to at the fourth Nigerian meeting held in Lagos, never functioned; only Congolese troops arrived, and then promptly left because of the danger and their own ineffectiveness.

Goukouni signed an agreement with Libya in June 1980 to gain support against Habré, and large numbers of Libyan troops began arriving at the end of the year as a surer source of support than the other foreign forces. In January 1981, Goukouni and Qaddafi jointly proclaimed the union of Libya and Chad, now under Libyan occupation. Pushed to the eastern border areas, Habré began receiving military aid from the United States through the CIA via Egypt and the Sudan. At the 1981 OAU summit in Nairobi, Kenya in June, African states revived the notion of an Inter-African Force, and pressures for the force grew in subsequent months, culminating in October in a direct appeal for its constitution by the French President with support from the United States. At the end of the month, Goukouni requested the withdrawal of the Libyan troops, and by the end of the year, the Inter-African Force of Nigerian, Senegalese, and Zairean troops was stationed across the middle of the country. But the mission of the OAU force was a vague task of "peacekeeping," its mandate lasted only to the end of June when free elections were to have been held, and Habré's FAN continued to make inroads into government defenses.

French and Libyan Intervention

Habré's takeover of the capital, the withdrawal of the IAF, and the dispersal of resistance in mid-1982 appeared to mark the end of the rebellion and the establishment of a consolidated central authority over the country for the first time in many years. Habré showed unsuspected statesmanship in negotiating with various factions, notably in the south, and in bringing in broad support behind his government. He was recognized by the OAU and the United Nations as the successor to the GUNT, and French and American economic aid was provided for reconstruction. However, the consolidation left two external spoilers— Goukouni and Qaddafi. In the attempts to hold an OAU summit in 1982, the Chadian question was kept alive by Libya, and when the summit was finally held in Addis Ababa in June 1983 and Mengistu Haile Mariam of Ethiopia was chosen to preside rather than Qaddafi, the Libyan leader left in a huff and stormed back to Tripoli to unleash Goukouni's forces. The Libyan Army and a smaller group of Chadian rebels attacked in July 1983 and, after being initially repulsed, occupied the northern half of the country. The United States avoided direct intervention but urged French support for Habré's government; Washington prepared to provide military coordination from the Sudan and Egypt through the use of AWACs planes. France, however, delayed, and only under strong African pressure finally intervened in August, holding the Libyan invasion to the northern half of the country. Zairean troops also were sent but stayed in the capital area. Nevertheless, the stalemate held into 1985.

During 1983, his second year in power, Habré continued to consolidate his support in the south and held his position internationally. The factionalism so characteristic of Chadian politics destroyed the solidarity of Goukouni's rebels, and Libya began to find its operations in northern Chad more expensive than its falling oil revenues could bear. France patiently continued to press for a new settlement on the basis of the variously interpreted slogan that had surfaced frequently in discussions of the conflict—withdrawal of all foreign forces. In September 1984, France and Libya announced an agreement based on an interpretation that provided for French withdrawal from the country, Libyan withdrawal to the `Aouzou strip, and maintenance of Zairean troops in the country.

Amidst much suspicion and uncertainty, the two forces began withdrawal. The Libyans did not go very far, but the French forces left the country, having accomplished their minimal purpose of stopping the Libyan invasion but leaving the country divided, with half still occupied by Libya. Chadian factions were unable to meet to establish reconciliation, but the Chadian conflict returned—for the moment—to its original internal dimension. Final resolution depends on the Chadian government's finding and allocating sufficient resources to keep the various contending factions satisfied and on the support of neighboring and external powers for the central government and their abstention from the backing of dissident factions. Unfortunately, even when each of these circles of conflict plays its role constructively, the danger still exists that the government will become a dominating clique headed by an irresponsible strongman, using its resources and support to oppress rather than to satisfy. Africa has known both sorts of conflict outcomes— political collapse and overpowering consolidation.

Differing Interests

Interests differ in each circle of the conflict. Each of the Chadian parties has an interest in seeing that its region receives a fair share of the benefits of independence, but personal interests of the factional leaders are also involved as each seeks adequate political rewards for his efforts in the rebellion. On the level of neighboring states, each state has an interest in seeing the Chadian vacuum filled with a competent authority, lest the vacuum attract another neighbor's interference or spread its dissidence to neighboring regions. Only Libya seems to have further interest; Qaddafi wants his unsupported claim to the 'Aouzou Strip recognized and legitimized, his union with the neighboring Moslem region in at least northern Chad consummated, and his base for the subversion of the Sudan, Niger, and possibly Nigeria consolidated. The African membership in the OAU has a strong interest in preventing Chad from becoming a precedent of collapse, aggression, annexation, and the defeat of regional peacekeeping forces; Chad is the first case in the continent of the unilateral annexation of a neighboring sovereign state's territory and of the military invasion of a neighboring sovereign state with intent to absorb it.

Outside of Africa, French interests concern a return to normalcy of an area of economic production and political responsibility. France is seen as the last resort for problems of political order and security by other Francophone African states in West and Central Africa, and France feels a continuing moral responsibility for stability in its former colony. The United States and the Soviet Union have no direct interests in the country. To the extent that Africa is a nonaligned part of the free world, with ties of economic, cultural, and political values primarily to the West, a collapse of order and security in Chad is seen as a problem for the West to solve. It is also seen as a problem that could attract unfriendly interference, although the chance of its attracting Soviet attention is farfetched.

Escalation

Analysts have made the distinction between intensification (doing more of the same) and escalation (doing something different), associating the latter with the crossing of "saliencies."[3] Saliencies in the Chadian conflict have involved moving from one circle of conflict to the next, and hence escalation has always been associated with external intervention. The analysis is complicated by the fact that the initial condition of the conflict involved the presence of foreign (French) troops as a residue of the colonial situation. Thereafter, various foreign interventions—notably Libyan and French troops, but also Nigerian and other African forces—all mark moments of escalation. Analysis is again complicated, however, by the fact that the sides are not equal in legitimacy. Although the ineptitude or oppressiveness of the central government was the basic cause of the rebellion, the government had at least a presumption of legitimacy in that it was the legitimate source of power that all sides sought to capture. Foreign forces—notably the French and the collective Africans, but also the Libyans on occasion—intervened to strengthen and at the same time to reform the central government, thus constituting a different sort of escalation than foreign intervention against the central government.

To Raise or To Call

Finally, escalation also took place to block the further extension (escalation) of the conflict or to check a previous escalation by the other side. Thus, one can talk of escalation to raise, escalation to call or to match, and escalation to raise again. Escalation to raise seeks to break out of a stalemate, whereas escalation to call seeks to create a stalemate. Until the French escalation of 1983, most interventions in the Chadian conflict were escalations to raise and to win. The type of interventions practiced by the various Inter-African Forces and by Nigeria is unclear, which is one of the reasons they were ineffective. In no case until 1983 was a foreign intervention an escalation to call, designed merely to keep one of the parties in the game so that the others would be obliged to deal with it. Only in 1983 did that become a foreign strategy, and it worked in a limited sort of way.

The saliencies that mark escalations can be thought of as "firebreaks," borders marking entry into new fields but also backstops against which containment can operate. The third circle of conflict fits this image particularly well. Superpower involvement has threat value as great as its perceived danger. None of the parties wants superpower intervention (except perhaps Habré, who on occasion can be arrogant in his righteousness), above all for fear of intervention by the other superpower. The Soviet Union has never intervened directly, although its arms sold to Libya are the military support for whichever side Libya is favoring. The United States was studiously uninterested in the conflict until 1981, when the advent of the Reagan administration in Washington and Libyan troops in Chad produced a new situation. American policy initially favored Habré, and US arms supplies gave him part of the means to hold out against Goukouni and then to begin to reverse the situation. (Habré also made extensive use of captured arms.) France appears to have been largely instrumental in convincing the United States to switch support to the Inter-African Force, and, contrary to some claims,[4] there is no evidence of covert US support for Habré after November 1981. Two years later, the United States was again reluctant to intervene directly in Chad, feeling that the conflict was properly the affair of the French (the second circle) and not the superpowers, although it was willing to provide military support for the FroLiNaT operations through AWACs and to provide economic support and military training for the recognized government.

Within the second and third circles of conflict, there are also two internal levels of escalation, marked by foreign aid and foreign troops. The passage from one to another marks an escalation, as seen in the introduction of French troops in 1968, 1977, and 1983, of Libyan troops in 1980 and 1983, and of American military aid in 1981 and 1983. Again, there is a problem of asymmetry: it seems that foreign aid to the established government is normal and does not constitute an escalation, whereas foreign aid to rebel movements is escalatory. In the case of foreign troops, an escalation seems to be involved whether the troops are supporting the government or the rebels.

The Escalation Process

With these conceptual distinctions as tools, the escalation process in the Chadian conflict can be analyzed. In the Tombalbaye period (1960–1975), escalations in support of FroLiNaT involved external support, above all Libyan after Qaddafi's coming to power in 1969. Such escalations were designed to keep the rebels in the conflict, not necessarily to provide the final push to victory, and as such the limited aim was rather easy to attain. Militarily, the rebellion was impossible to put down, either by the Chadian Army or by foreign armies, as long as it had a bit of support through arms supplies from neighboring countries. Elements in the rebellion were the basic northern grievances, rivalry for power among northern leaders, a tradition of dissidence, and knowledge of the terrain; all gave an impetus and an advantage to the rebellion. Escalation in support of the government involved external support— including troops—from France, which was doomed to ineffectiveness since it could overcome neither the elements of the internal revolt nor the support from the outside. Once a new generation of FroLiNaT leaders came to the fore at the beginning of the 1970's, with different regions to represent in their grievances against the government, their rivalries actually helped keep the rebellion alive, since even when some were bought off, others would keep up the fight with foreign aid.

In the Malloum period (1975–1978), Libyan aid continued and the return of the French again proved ineffective, even with the attempt to form a Great Coalition in the Habré-Malloum government. This move was carried to its conclusion in the GUNT, where a full Great Coalition of all eleven factions was formed. But the internal conflict continued: the factions could not rule together, but no one of them could rule alone. Escalation through Libyan intervention, now in support of Goukouni in the government, was met with an international outcry and also proved ineffective, in part because Habré in turn was able to obtain support from abroad. The tables were turned in 1983, when Goukouni was in the rebellion and Habré in the government. Escalation from the two main sources of external support—Libya and France, respectively—caused a stalemate, effective this time because the only way to break out of it would have been a direct military confrontation between the two armies, with the French in the stronger position militarily and in terms of legitimacy. At the same time, Habré worked to overcome the internal conflict by negotiating with forces within his territory.

In sum, no conceivable escalation—short of major-power involvement—was capable of assuring government victory throughout the 1960's and 1970's so long as intervention from neighbors was available to keep the rebellion alive. Similarly, no escalation in favor of the rebels could assure their permanent victory so long as support for their opponents was available from the outside unless neighboring supporters for the rebellion were willing to occupy the country. The latter option was tried in 1981 and abandoned because of cost. Therefore, for the conflict to be overcome, a stalemate and a mutual disengagement had to take place between competing intervenors, and a national leader had to emerge who could both win and reconcile. To the extent that any of these elements was imperfectly realized, the conflict resolution was incomplete. In the event, total reconciliation had still not taken place by 1985, leaving Goukouni weak but still a potential source of further conflict. The Libyan evacuation had not occurred, leaving both the 'Aouzou Strip and the larger north occupied and effectively integrated into Libya. Yet Habré has emerged as the winner and ruler over what remains of Chad.

There has never been any question of superpower confrontation nor of direct intervention by either superpower.

Management

A solution to the Chadian conflict requires the installation of a central government with the will and the means to attend to the needs of the various regions of the country. It also requires support for that government from neighboring and external states, including superpowers, through tangible assistance and legitimization and through abstention from any support for rebellious movements. Essentially, resolution of the conflict depends, at the core, on the appearance of a central government force or figure who will act responsively toward the population and not perpetuate the real grievances that underlay the conflict in the first place. Thus, conflict-resolution measures that defeat the rebellion but that do not meet its grievances are inadequate, and even conflict-management measures that check or eliminate the means of conflict—the usual notion of conflict management—will not last long if they are not also tied to responsible governance. Since the conflict concerns Chad, where the qualities of generosity and statesmanship are in short supply and the means of satisfying real as well as political needs are equally scarce, the chances of a lasting resolution of the conflict and the successful building of a cohesive nation are slim.

Conflict management has been further hindered by the fact that during much of its history the conflict has never provided the constraints of a stalemate to compel the parties to come to an agreement to either limit or resolve. The opportunity has therefore always been present for any party to seek outside support to escalate in the belief that it could win. This was the situation all through the Tombalbaye and Malloum periods. None of the FroLiNaT factions had any incentive to come to terms because they had little to lose by fighting, little to gain by coming to terms with the central government, and everything to gain in keeping up the pressure on the government—since every time France intervened, it pressed reforms on Ndjamena. The situation began to change in 1979, when FroLiNaT victory paradoxically brought a stalemate because of the factional nature of the rebellion. Before the formation of the GUNT, all factions had had the same interest in coming together to establish a government collectively, namely, that each individually could share in power. As outs, they had a collective interest in getting in, overriding any separate interests. This they did during the four Nigerian conferences in 1979. However, once the GUNT was established, each faction had an interest in striking out alone, provided it could find some outside backing, and so the same weakness obtained as during the previous period. As ins, each had a separate interest in monopolizing power and driving the others out, if that was possible. In the GUNT, all factions were victorious, and none was defeated as a faction (not even the faction representing the south).

Options for Effective Government

With the formation of the GUNT, the needs of conflict management changed and became more complicated. Since the breakaway option still existed (and indeed was practiced by Habré and by others to a lesser extent), conflict managers still had to be able to block escalation—to prevent any party from striking out alone with foreign support—in order to be effective. But conflict managers also had to provide a means for an effective exercise of power to be practiced by the GUNT as a government. The range of possibilities was broader than was generally recognized. It included a number of options: a decentralized federal system in which each faction controlled its fief under a weak central government, a collective central government under a dominant faction, and a majority government (coalition or single-faction) elected democratically on the basis of a competitive vote. In a moment of wild idealism, the OAU chose the last option, the least likely among difficult paths. In each case, some facilitating help was required from external conflict managers, including conference auspices and pressures, peace-keeping forces, election assistance, and other contributions, in addition to agreement by the Chadian parties to play by the newly established rules and not to strike out alone. Whether or not this requirement was too high in theory, it was too much in reality, and the GUNT collapsed when one or more of the factions bolted.

The latest pattern of conflict management was the creation of a stalemate among the external parties, allowing for their mutual withdrawal (from Chadian politics if not from Chadian territory) while the parties to the internal conflict fought to the finish. It was not necessary for all the factions to fight it out to the end; the strongest among them took on the task, alone or in coalition. Habré's FAN defeated Goukouni's FAP and then formed its own alliance against the splinters of the GUNT. Presumably, this development has taken care of the basic element that prevented any of the previous options from coming close to realization: a predominant, not necessarily solely victorious, faction restructured the balance of forces so that it, rather than simply interfactional cooperation, was able to enforce the newly established rules. The conclusion may be delicate, but it is important. Conflict managers can facilitate agreement and can remove external supports for conflict, but they cannot enforce positive agreement. When the conflict has caused the breakdown of central authority, conflict management cannot reconstruct that authority. While they can help set up the rules and procedures by which authority is reconstituted, conflict managers cannot invent an effective central leadership.

Means of Management

Outside of financial aid, there are four main means of conflict management that have been used in Chad: military intervention, peacekeeping forces, unilateral reform assistance, and mediation. These means were used, and others considered, by a wide range of agencies, including interested states (African, former colonial, and superpower) and organizations (regional, OAU; and global, UN). These will be evaluated in turn.

Military intervention against the rebellion was practiced on a number of occasions in three different ways. The French intervened in the early 1960's, in 1968–75, and in 1977–80 against the rebellion, and the Libyans can be considered to have done the same in 1981, although they saw little actual fighting. It is notable that interventions against the rebellion were not necessarily in support of the government; particularly the French tried to exact reforms from the government and to reconcile it with the rebels. Often these efforts were effective for a while: in 1960–65, in 1969–71, in 1973–74, and in 1981. But after a time, military intervention only provoked counter-interventions to raise, and the lulls in the fighting were never effectively used to work out a conciliation among the parties to the conflict. Lessons would be that:

1. *Military intervention to hold down a conflict must be accompanied by a program of reconciliation among the parties;*

2. *Military intervention in an internal conflict must be accompanied by diplomatic measures to seal off external support to the rebellion.*

The Libyans also intervened in 1983 on behalf of the rebellion, but this was scarcely a conflict-management measure. It was designed to escalate the rebellion to victory and to chase out Habré as he had chased out Goukouni the year before.

Military intervention was practiced in a different way by the French in 1983 to counter the Libyan invasion and to create a stalemate. As noted, this was a "calling" rather than a "raising" escalation, and combined with a number of other necessary but insufficient factors, it created the stalemate required for conflict management and perhaps resolution. Thus:

3. *Military intervention that creates a hurting stalemate, that threatens to lead to a much worse situation not desired by either side, is the effective basis for deescalation and conflict management.*

Peacekeeping forces to provide or restore order in lieu of effective government were introduced by Nigeria and France in 1979, provided by the Lagos agreements of 1979 but never deployed, provided again by the OAU in 1981, and withdrawn in confusion in 1982.[5] The Libyan forces of 1980–81 may also be considered to be unilateral peacekeeping forces, but the term is usually used to cover multinational forces with no interest in any particular side of the conflict. All peacekeeping forces in Chad were failures, although more because of the way they carried out their job than by their nature.

Admittedly the job is difficult, as the large literature on peacekeeping forces in general has pointed out.[6] It is more difficult in a conflict such as Chad where the job is not to establish a thin blue line that separates combatants, frustrates their combat, and forces them to turn (or to stick) to other means of pursuing relations on a nonmilitary level. In Chad, as in Zaire (formerly the Belgian Congo) earlier, the job was to provide law and order in a situation where the lines were not clear. The peacekeeping forces were supposed to protect the capital area in particular. However, in the largest multinational exercise, in 1981, to Goukouni's frustration and dismay, it was never clear whether the Inter-African Force was to defend the government, as the substitute for a collapsing national army, or to protect the Chadian population while the factions worked out their political relations around it. When it turned out that Goukouni no longer had the support of the factions in the GUNT and had become the head of a faction or a group of factions again, the peacekeeping force could no longer both stay above factional politics and maintain law and order in the capital, the two things it was supposed to do. It folded its tents and slipped away under the cover of an administrative deadline.

Had its orders been clearer, had the ultimate conflict-resolution mechanism (elections) been a realistic and feasible option within the allotted time, and had the breakaway option been kept closed, the OAU's Inter-African Force would have had the conditions necessary to accomplish its task. But only when the parties to the conflict had decided to follow the rules of a realistic conflict-resolving mechanism could a small international force keep order and represent authority in a country as vast and difficult as Chad. The lesson is clear:

4. *A peacekeeping force can perform only minimal law-and-order functions and can do so only when the parties are agreed not to challenge or to circumvent it in that role. It is unlikely that the members of a peacekeeping force will feel their interests affected enough to take the heavy casualties required to impose a solution or to contain a conflict if the parties have the will and the means to pursue it.*

Reform measures are a necessary adjunct to conflict management and were pressed on the Chadian government by the French in 1969 and 1983 and by the Libyans in 1972. The returns are not yet in on current efforts, but the earlier attempts failed. The simplest answer is that reforms are necessary but not sufficient; once conflict has reached a level serious enough for the parties to see their interest in sustained fighting, they are unlikely to be appeased by mere reforms. Yet even without the proof of success, it can be noted that decentralization and local autonomy, as advised in 1969 and 1983 and neglected in 1972, are important approaches to reform in the case of regional and ethnic conflict. Somehow, governments fear that local autonomy will lead to secession; yet Africa and the Middle East, and probably other areas as well, suffer much more from local rebellions against the heavy hand of central government than from secessionists trying to turn autonomy into independence. In conclusion:

5. *Reform, notably the return of local affairs to local hands and the meeting of local allocative needs, is as necessary to the resolution of conflict as is the control of the means of escalation.*

Mediation became part of the conflict-management efforts after a decade of conflict had shown that the conflict was there to stay and the parties legitimate enough in their grievances to be recognized as part of the solution. France pressed for a coalition of government and opposition in 1978, African states mediated in 1979 and desultorily thereafter, and France mediated intensively in 1983–84. The Chadian experience heavily underlines the basic ingredients necessary for successful mediation: stalemate as a context, and then legitimacy, leverage, and stake as characteristics of the mediator. Stalemate was present at all three times, but most strongly in the last effort, when the mediator itself was holder of the stalemate. The case shows clearly a point that is only coming to be understood: that the mediator need not be disinterested and impartial and that it may well even be engaged on the side of one of the parties, but that it must be able to produce an outcome that is preferable to the present and foreseeable future for both (all) sides.[7]

Thus, leverage can be linked to stalemate, but it is also associated with the ability of the mediator to deliver—above all to deliver an acceptable outcome but also to deliver the agreement of the side with which it is most closely associated. Leverage of this sort was available to the mediators in the late 1970's only if they were not pushed and challenged, whereas France was in a much stronger position by virtue of its own direct engagement in 1983. Legitimacy was available both to France, because of its postcolonial status, and to the African states. However, almost anyone else who wanted to try a hand at mediation and had the other characteristics would doubtless have been acceptable. Stake (interest by the mediator in a solution) is also clearly important in the degree of leverage a mediator is willing to exercise. Objectively, one might think that African states would have a greater interest in a Chadian solution, although France had its postcolonial reputation and responsibility at issue. However, the African states felt vulnerable to the pressures that the various parties and their allies could bring on them, and the Africans lost their ability to press the parties to come to a solution. France was closely enough engaged and far enough away to have both leverage and detachment.

As noted, to say whether the French succeeded or failed depends on a definition of the goals. As both mediator and counterescalator, France was able to negotiate its own withdrawal in late 1984 without inviting a Libyan advance but without securing a Libyan retreat, either. France was hoodwinked in the process, having announced that Libya too would withdraw, and Libya showed itself to be as untrustworthy as many suspected. In another sense, however, France accomplished for the moment by diplomacy what it had orginally done more expensively by military means—it held Libyan troops in check. Thus, the most negative part of the outcome—its most striking failure—was not its inability to support the new government in its restoration of authority over half the country but its throwing away of the bargaining chip that would have allowed it to recover control over the rest of Chad. Since the French government perceived that it had a greater stake in its own withdrawal than in a Chadian solution (mutual withdrawal), France lost the stalemate that it had created and therefore its leverage. (Foreign Minister Claude Cheysson also lost his job for having presided over the unequal trade.)

The lessons of the case show what is necessary for successful mediation, but they also show that the qualities are hard to create if not present:

6. *A mediator must have legitimacy, leverage, and stakes—these three, but the greatest of these is leverage, the ability to produce a broadly acceptable outcome;*

7. *A stalemate is the necessary context for mediation, in which the mediator helps the parties find an outcome preferable to the mess they are in;*

8. *Mediators may need to enforce the stalemate if one does not occur naturally in order to strengthen their leverage;*

9. *Leverage is not a matter of making a party agree by purchase or pressure, but of producing an attractive outcome.*

Agents of Management

Finally, the agents of conflict management can be evaluated. The superpowers did well to stay out, and the United States did well to insist that France, in the absence of the African states, should handle the affair in the end, although the United States did not convey its insistence very well. On the other hand, it is hard to fault either superpower for providing aid to the government, resources of any kind being so scarce in Chad. More debatable was the covert support for Habré in 1981. The American official fixation on Qaddafi as the local whipping boy, portrayed as a powerful satan, was clearly out of place; but in the middle of 1981, with Libyan troops in Chad, no OAU action in view, and a weak leader of the GUNT unable to hold his factions together, it is understandable that the United States gave support to the one factional leader who looked like he might be able to provide strong central leadership to the country. In addition, under the current conventions of superpower conduct in Africa, such aid was not likely to provoke a confrontation between the two powers.

The former metropole had a role to play. It is important to note that expectations of French action came above all, not from a globalist cold warrior or a nostalgic neocolonialist, but from African presidents of neighboring French-speaking countries. As noted, France combined the characteristics of interest, leverage, and distance, and in addition it was known to be a reluctant intervenor or an intervenor in extremis. Its eagerness to leave made its willingness to intervene acceptable.

African states individually were potentially acceptable as conflict managers, the more so to the extent that they embodied the same virtues as France. Thus, neighbors were basically unwelcome, as both Nigeria and Libya found, and powerful neighbors were more unwelcome than others. Togo for a while was a helpful mediator; Nigeria was also, to be sure, but it lost its welcome when it came too close. Members of the various Inter-African Forces were all non-neighbors, except for Nigeria. For the most part, African states individually were too weak to play any more than a purely facilitating or communicating version of a mediator's role.

African states collectively, including their organized form in the OAU, had an important role to play, and they failed sadly to live up either to their ideals or to their interests. Three groups of states were notable failures. Chad's neighbors, grouped together, could have joined at some point in the late 1970's to pledge nonintervention behind any particular rebel faction and to impose on the parties the need for an end to the conflict. Had Nigeria, the Sudan, Libya, and Cameroon agreed to such a demarche and stuck with it, they would have had a good chance of success. As it was, they took the first steps in the Nigerian meetings of 1979 but then lost hope, while one of them intervened directly. Sustained, committed action was not a characteristic of African states in the 1980's.

The second group of African states that failed its responsibilities was the collection of proposed contributors to the Inter-African Forces— Guinea, Benin, the Congo, Nigeria, Zaire, and Senegal. The first three never arrived to fulfill their obligations in 1979 (Congolese troops got to Ndjamena but then turned around and went home), marking the beginning of the collapse of the Lagos agreements. In the absence of precise instructions from the OAU, the second three were unable to unite on a clear notion of their mandate, agreeing in the end only on the need to leave by the end of June 1982. In leaving—and in not arriving in the first place—they carried off with them the OAU expectations of a precedent for African peacekeeping forces that would have been useful for other conflicts.

The third group that failed was the OAU itself. It took long periods of time to come to any agreement on action to take in Chad, gave unclear instructions to its agents, and was generally paralyzed by its fear of encroaching on a member's internal affairs or even on the sovereign right of other members to decide on their own policy. In the end, one weakness leading to another, it even defaulted on its obligation to uphold colonially inherited borders and to denounce military invasion by a neighboring country. There is no remedy for such failure other than for African leaders to become more aware of their responsibilities.

The United Nations had little to do with the Chadian conflict. Both global and regional members agreed that it should be handled by the OAU, and the one time that it came to the United Nations it was quickly sent back to the OAU. This was probably the best result: the United Nations is ill-suited to the task of reestablishing central authority, and the only state with enough interest to supply a peacekeeping force was France, which was present anyhow. At the end of 1981, an OAU appeal to the Security Council and the Secretary General for unspecified help with its Inter-African Force received no response both because of its vagueness and because it did not come from the government of Chad. When Goukouni did make the request, in April 1982, he was no longer recognized by the OAU. The Security Council responded the following month by establishing a voluntary fund for assistance to the IAF; however, the force itself withdrew the next month. Habré appealed to the United Nations on several occasions after that, but the Security Council took no action.

Thus, there were two possible roles for the United Nations: direct support or intervention, and indirect support for the OAU. In the event, the world body provided neither. In abstaining from the first, it was doubtless correct: Security Council members sent the issue back to the OAU under the slogan, "African solutions for African problems." They should have done so with more forcefulness, for the OAU took clear steps in Chad (the sending of the IAF) only when prodded from the outside. In abstaining from the second, the system rather than the United Nations itself was at fault. There is no provision in UN procedures for responding to a call for a peacekeeping force when it does not come from the government concerned, for to do otherwise would be direct intervention in internal affairs. The concern is valid, but appropriate procedures need to be developed. Furthermore, the OAU did not specify— and probably did not know—what help it needed, although at the same time, the United Nations Secretariat and the OAU Implementation Committee were cooperating closely on technical support for another similar matter—conflict resolution through referendum and peacekeeping forces in Western Sahara. (Here again, it was the OAU that aborted its role, in February 1982.) Procedures need also to be developed for technical support from one international organization to the other. The lesson here:

10. *The United Nations needs to develop procedures for technical cooperation with regional organizations for peacekeeping and conflict-resolution contingencies.*

Notes

1. For other basic works on Chad, see Robert Buijtenhuijs, *Le FroLiNaT et les revoltes populaires du Chad* (The Hague: Mouton, 1978); Virginia Thompson and Richard Adloff, *Conflict in Chad* (Berkeley: University of California Institute of International Studies, 1981); Samuel Decalo, *Historical Dictionary of Chad* (Metuchen: Scarecrow, 1977); Samuel Decalo, "Regionalism, Political Decay, and Civil Strife in Chad," XVIII *Journal of Modern African Studies* 1:23–56 (1980); and Alex Rondos, "Why Chad?" CSIS *Africa Notes* 18 (1983).

2. See Dean Pittman, "The OAU and Chad" in Yassin El-Ayouty and I. William Zartman, eds., *The OAU After Twenty Years* (New York: Praeger, 1984).

3. See Thomas Schelling, *The Strategy of Conflict* (Cambridge: Harvard University Press, 1960); Richard Smoke, *War: Controlling Escalation* (Cambridge: Harvard University Press, 1979); and I. William Zartman, *Ripe for Resolution: Conflict and Intervention in Africa* (New York: Oxford University Press, 1985).

4. See the good discussion in Jay Peterzell, "The Secret War Against Qaddafi," *The Nation*, January 22, 1984.

5. See Pittman and Henry Wiseman, "Peacekeeping and Conflict Resolution" in El-Ayouty and Zartman, eds., *The OAU After Twenty Years*; and Nathan Pelkovits, "Peacekeeping: The African Experience" in Henry Wiseman, ed., *Peacekeeping: Appraisals and Proposals* (New York: Pergamon, 1983).

6. Among others, see, most recently, Wiseman, *Peacekeeping*; Indar Rikhye, *Theory and Practice of Peacekeeping* (London: Hurst, 1984); Indar Rikhye et al., *The Thin Blue Line* (New Haven: Yale University Press, 1974); and *The Peacekeeper's Handbook* (New York: International Peace Academy, 1978).

7. For this point and for an analysis of the mediation process, see Saadia Touval and I. William Zartman, eds., *International Mediation in Theory and Practice* (Boulder, Colorado: Westview Press, 1985), especially "International Mediation: Conflict Resolution and Power Politics."

II

Civil Conflict in Lebanon

Arthur R. Day

Introduction

The Lebanese civil conflict that began in 1975 provides an excellent case study in escalation and in forms of intervention ranging widely in scale and purpose. This relatively obscure dispute over domestic power-sharing has been closely intertwined with international conflicts and tensions that, in turn, have had serious consequences for the entire Middle East and have affected the interests of the superpowers as well. While the explosive force of this train of conflicts was unusual, the basic situation was not. Throughout the world there are domestic tensions that, should they erupt into major violence, would threaten to involve outside states that see their interests affected. Thus, the Lebanese pattern could be repeated elsewhere. The case is of general interest as well because most of the available forms of intervention, political and military, mischievous and constructive, large- and small-scale, have been employed. Their results provide food for thought about ways of dealing with future conflicts.

In studying the Lebanon example, the two most important questions to ask are: what kinds of results seem most achievable by outside intervention; and what forms of intervention seem most effective in producing these results? In analyzing the first question, we will be interested to know whether interventions have much success in resolving disputes or whether they seem most effective in achieving results short of resolution—stopping hostilities, moderating the severity of fighting, limiting the spread of a conflict to new areas or new participants, and so forth. In studying the forms of intervention, we shall look at actions by individual governments, by ad hoc groups of states, and by multilateral organizations, both regional and global. In attempting to interpret the

Arthur R. Day is senior consultant to the United Nations Association of the USA. He was formerly in the American Foreign Service, and served from 1975 to 1977 as Deputy Assistant Secretary of State for Near Eastern and South Asian Affairs. He is the author of a forthcoming book on Jordan.

complexity of a situation such as Lebanon and to find useful lessons for the future, the questions might resolve themselves into a single inquiry: what forms of intervention are most effective in achieving what kinds of results? The answers might suggest that there are no simple answers, that different means are appropriate to different situations.

Escalation

Setting the Stage for Escalation

The centuries-long history of Lebanon, but especially the experience of the post–World War II years, made it inevitable that a serious domestic conflict would involve outside players. The country was a mosaic of religious sects and family-based clans, virtually all of which had close ties beyond Lebanon's borders. In some cases, these ties had been cultivated by the Lebanese factions to enhance their power in competition with other factions; in other cases, the factions were simply the Lebanese branch, so to speak, of broad-based political or religious groups whose loyalties were engaged in the fate of Lebanese brethren. A variety of states saw their interests affected by developments in Lebanon, beginning with the neighboring states of Syria and Israel and extending out to Iraq, Saudi Arabia, Egypt, and beyond. *Washington Post* correspondent Jonathan Randall may exaggerate when he says that "virtually every politician was on the take from some foreign power, if not several,"[1] but Lebanon was certainly a very permeable system. And finally, another bitter conflict—that of the Palestinians and the Israelis—was intricately interlaced with Lebanon's domestic tensions. Lebanon was neither another 1930's Spain nor a pre-1914 Europe waiting for Sarajevo, but some of the qualities of both made it a flammable mixture that would not burn in isolation.

The Maronites. It was the Maronites, the largest Christian sect, who most felt the need for support outside Lebanon. Feeling themselves doubly a minority—Christians in a Moslem world, a Roman sect in an Eastern Orthodox majority (some Maronites even considered themselves non-Arabs)—they turned for protection to Catholic France as early as the seventeenth century. They renounced the formal backing of the French as a condition for the National Pact of 1943, which was the basis for the independent Lebanese state.[2] When they subsequently felt their position threatened by a Moslem challenge in the late 1950's, they began to consider Israel as a possible substitute. They also made persistent but largely unsuccessful efforts to engage the United States on their behalf.

Most of the other communities, or groups within them, had support from outside governments. In no other case, however, was it such a preoccupation, or so fateful in its consequences, as it was with the Maronites.

The Palestinians. The situation of the Palestinians was very different. They were actors from outside the country who were playing out a quite separate drama on the crowded Lebanese stage. By virtue of their very presence, however, and because of the way they pursued their own goals, they helped create the conditions for the civil war and became deeply involved in it when it broke out.

The Palestinian movement began to take significant form after the 1967 war and was initially quite widely supported in Lebanon. As the Palestinians began to operate against Israel, however, and to attract more and more devastating Israeli retaliation upon Lebanon, their presence and activities hastened the polarization of Moslem and Maronite opinion. This situation raised in an especially dramatic way the old question of Lebanon's "Arabness." Israeli attacks such as the 1968 destruction of Lebanon's commercial air fleet at Beirut airport were intended to force the Lebanese government to control the Palestinians. The Christian right, especially the Maronites, wanted to come down hard on the Palestinians, while the Moslem left believed that the army should be defending the country against Israel, not attacking fellow Arabs. From then until the civil war broke out, Palestine Liberation Organization (PLO) forces, at times supported by sympathetic Lebanese militias, clashed again and again with the army, itself at times supported by right-wing militias.

The Maronites came to feel more and more threatened by forces, mainly of the Moslem left, that wanted basic changes in the economic and political order. They believed that the Palestinians provided a powerful stimulus to this movement and at the same time gave it a military strength, through the PLO militias, that it could not muster alone. Kamal Jumblat, the Druse leader until his assassination in 1977, was quoted early in the civil war as saying, "The Lebanese army is the Christians' army, and the Palestinian resistance is the Moslems' army."[3] However that may have been, the Maronites began seriously building up their militias well before the civil war, mainly as a response to Palestinian strength.

Regional States. Beyond the borders of Lebanon, the states that saw their interests as most deeply affected by Lebanese developments were the neighboring states of Syria and Israel. For Syria, of course, there was the recollection of a common past, and for some Syrians perhaps, the hope for a common future in a "Greater Syria." More immediately, however, Lebanon as seen from Damascus was a society that interacted at many levels with Syrian society, whose sectarian discord could infect Syria's own fragile ethnic and religious balance. It was, moreover, a fertile field where Syria's Middle East enemies encouraged and financed movements to embarrass the government in Damascus. The struggle between the Palestinian resistance and the Israeli forces across Lebanon's southern border also posed the latent threat of an unwanted Syrian confrontation with Israel. Syria was concerned at the continuing prospect of the partition of Lebanon between Christian and Moslem areas, advocated by some Christians, which it saw as giving Israel the opportunity to seize the Lebanese south. Oddly enough though, in retrospect, Egypt under Gamal Abdel Nasser played a greater role in Lebanese affairs than did Syria in the period prior to the civil war. It was Egypt, for example, that acted as the broker for the 1969 understanding on the status of the Palestinian resistance in Lebanon (the so-called Cairo Agreement).

Israel's principal concern regarding Lebanon was that the country not serve as a base for hostile activity by the Palestinian resistance, by indigenous Moslem elements, or by Syria. It intervened repeatedly with military force after 1967 not only to strike at the PLO directly but to so punish the Lebanese as to make them inhospitable to the PLO's presence and activity. It was important for Israeli purposes that the Maronites remain the dominant ruling element in Lebanon and indeed that the Maronite-controlled government and army be strong enough to control the Palestinians and also to resist the pressures from Arab governments to join the conflict against Israel. The Israelis thus had an interest in the indigenous political situation in Lebanon as well as in their separate war with the Palestinians.

Of the other countries in the region, Egypt, Iraq, and Libya had the most active fingers in the Lebanese pie. Egypt under Anwar Sadat found it difficult to surrender to Syria the predominance it had enjoyed in the great days of Nasser. Iraq missed no opportunity to weaken or harass its Baathist rival and bitter opponent, Hafez al-Assad's Syria. Libya saw the promise of a Moslem state in Lebanon and also the opportunity to attack Egypt's policy and image. All three of these countries financed leftist Moslem groups and their militias, Libya contributing by 1967 an amount estimated at $30 to $40 million to Lebanese politicians, militias, and anti-Egyptian newspapers.[4]

Superpowers. Wide regional involvement in a serious Lebanese conflict was thus assured. The same was not the case with the superpowers. Despite the stubborn Maronite assumption that the United States stood ready to assist them, top-level administration officials had little interest in Lebanon per se in the years prior to the civil war. Even the 1958 intervention was directed primarily against what were seen as broad regional radical trends, not at Lebanese internal convolutions. The interest level was so low, in fact, that American officials did not make the efforts they should have made at that critical time to disabuse the Maronites of their dangerous delusion. It was left for Ambassador G. McMurtrie Godley, in the first year of the civil war, to attempt to do so; he had only limited success. Here was a curious case of an intervention that had no substance in fact or intention playing a very real psychological role in a regional crisis.

The Soviet Union, it appeared, had even less interest in Lebanon. Moscow's principal link with the Lebanese problem was the PLO, which it supported and armed. There were two pro-Moscow Communist parties in the country—the Lebanese Communist party and the Communist Action Organization. They attracted support among the Shiites—the Moslem sect at the bottom of the economic ladder—until the PLO and the Shiites' own Movement of the Deprived (Amal) provided more aggressive channels for Shiite revolutionary purposes. Their relations with Moscow became strained as younger leaders espoused a type of Marxist Arab nationalism. Moscow received little benefit and enjoyed little influence through either of them. Neither the United States nor the Soviet Union seemed to regard Lebanon as of vital interest in itself or as an inseparable part of the broader Middle East complex that was the object of competition between them. It was a sideshow, despite all the many Middle East political currents that ran through it. Prior to the outbreak of the civil war, most of the issues that were being played out so intensely in Lebanon were not seen in either capital as significantly affecting its interests in the region.

Civil War: Outbreak and Escalation

By 1975, the political, social, and economic fabric of Lebanon was in shreds. It was widely accepted that Christian political domination no longer reflected the population makeup, in which the Moslems were now thought to constitute roughly 60 percent, heavily augmented by Palestinian refugees and Syrian workers. Public acceptance of the distribution of political power established by the National Pact of 1943 had dissipated, although the 1943 formula continued to determine the makeup of the government throughout the conflict. The Christians, the Maronites in particular, convinced that their security depended on their remaining in control, felt deeply threatened. The main-line Sunni Moslems, who had shared power with the Christians, saw the marked increase in Shiite numbers and a new political assertiveness of the Shiite community as a threat to their position. The Lebanese economy was booming, but the poor increased in numbers and in privation, with tens of thousands, mostly Shiites, driven off the land into urban slums by technological development and unremitting Israeli attacks in the largely Shiite south. Inflation was high; strikes and workers' riots occurred.

The most serious damage to the country's fragile domestic balance probably came from outside, however. The development of large and heavily armed Palestinian militias and the continuing and devastating Israeli raids magnified and accelerated the centrifugal process in Lebanese society. Tensions between the Maronites and the Palestinians were high.

Outbreak. Not suprisingly, therefore, the civil war began with an incident between Palestinians and the principal Maronite militia, the Phalange. On Sunday, April 13, 1975, gunmen, never identified, fired at the party of Pierre Gemayel, the Phalange chieftain, outside a Maronite church. A bodyguard and two others were killed. In classic Lebanese fashion, Phalange militiamen thereupon ambushed a bus carrying twenty-eight passengers, mostly Palestinians, killing all of them.

Almost at once, the incident escalated into a broad political and military confrontation. Fighting broke out between the Maronite militias on the one side, and, on the other, some of the Palestinian militias and the various components of the National Movement, a loose confederation of leftist Moslem forces under the leadership of Druse chieftain Jumblat. At this stage, however, and for several months to come, the Palestinians involved in the fighting belonged to the smaller, more radical militias. PLO leader Yasir Arafat held back from the conflict the forces of his own faction, Al Fatah, the largest of the PLO militias. He argued that the role of the PLO in Lebanon was to fight the Israelis, not to take sides among the Lebanese.

As the fighting intensified in the following months, so did the interplay between the domestic combatants and those foreign governments that believed that they had a stake in its outcome, or in its continuation. In the fall of 1975, for example, the Phalange (it is said, with Egyptian support), feeling beleaguered, called for the intervention of the Arab League. Two months later, on December 16, President Suleiman Franjieh called on the Syrians to redress the balance in favor of the Maronites.

By January 1976, however, without any Syrian assistance, the Maronites had mounted major offensives, mainly against Palestinian targets. A Moslem counteroffensive bogged down, and it was the turn of Jumblat's National Movement to appeal to Damascus. Syria sent to Lebanon the 3,500-man Yarmuk brigade of the Palestinian Liberation Army (the PLA, not the PLO) that had been stationed in Syria. Their introduction enabled the Moslems to press home their attacks. The January Phalange offensive against the Palestinians had another and more ominous consequence. It, together with a general concern about the viability of the leftist Moslem forces, led Arafat in early 1976 to commit the bulk of the PLO forces to the support of the National Movement. He feared that a Maronite victory over the Lebanese left would leave the Palestinians as the next target, a target that, in these circumstances, would stand alone. In this judgment he was very likely correct. A major external force was thus thrown onto the scales. The Fatah regular forces totaled 8,000–10,000 men, with about the same number of militia, compared to about 15,000 in the Maronite Phalange. The balance tipped sharply against the Christians, whose position became increasingly threatened.

The point should be made at this stage that an important dimension of the conflict is being omitted here in order to develop it more fully in the next section on efforts by outside actors to end the fighting and to resolve the dispute. Syria had commenced an active political campaign in September 1975 to arrange a cease-fire and ultimately to negotiate a new distribution of power in Lebanon to replace the outmoded National Pact. Syrian reinforcement of one side or the other was intended in part to create a balance that would encourage agreement among the parties.

The maneuvering among the players, domestic and foreign, at this stage is illustrative of the intense interplay between the local and regional factions. As the Syrians asserted greater control in Lebanon in the late winter and spring of 1976 and swung their support toward the weakening Christians while increasing pressure on the PLO and the Lebanese left, Arafat began to look to the Egyptians for backing against Syria. This required considerable refurbishment of ties with Cairo. The PLO had excoriated Sadat after the second Egyptian-Israeli disengagement agreement the year before. But now Arafat was doubly worried. He not only needed support in Lebanon, but he was concerned as well about a developing rapprochement between Syria and Jordan, seeing in it the possible seeds of a West Bank settlement at the expense of the PLO. The Egyptians, for their part, were only too happy to reinforce Arafat's capacity to stand up to their bitter rivals, the Syrians. They sent to Lebanon for this purpose, in early 1976, a PLA unit stationed in Egypt, despite the fact that for months they had been supporting the Maronites. The Iraqis, also anxious to strike at the Syrians, transferred to Lebanon at about the same time a PLA unit that had been stationed in Iraq.

During this same period, Israel began more open and intensive support of the Christian right, principally the Phalange. Large-scale supply of weaponry by Israel and the training of Christian fighters, partly in Israel, helped the Christian side hold out through the spring until the Syrians intervened in force.

Syrian Invasion. Syrian efforts to control the Lebanese situation through the gradual introduction of their own PLA units and Saiqa forces (a Syrian-sponsored PLO militia) proved insufficient. On June 1, 1976, therefore, Assad moved large contingents of Syrian Army forces across the border. By June 7, he had 12,000 troops in Lebanon equipped with armor, and ultimately the force amounted to 25,000–30,000 men. Almost from the outset, the Syrians had to fight their way in against Palestinian and Moslem left resistance.

The Syrian move, whatever its purpose, thus amounted to a substantial escalation of the conflict in terms of both its magnitude and intensity, and the number of active players. It contained the risk, moreover, of a far greater escalation to a Syrian-Israeli war, since Israel was certain to be uneasy about the presence of Syrian forces above its northern border. In the next section, the efforts that were made to avoid such a confrontation will be discussed. The fact that the Syrians had come in on the side of the Christians, whom the Israelis were by that time actively supporting with weapons and training, reduced the danger somewhat. Thus, for a period of time, the two regional powers were no longer backing opponents in the conflict. Nonetheless, with this move Syria had opened another front with Israel and had increased the chances for the outbreak of regional war. The Lebanese civil war had become a predominantly foreign conflict, with the Syrians and the Palestinians constituting the major elements on the opposing sides and with the Israelis exerting heavy pressure from the wings.

The Syrian escalation and the "internationalization" of the conflict helped prepare the way, however, for an Arab League cease-fire the following fall. It put the hitherto dominant National Movement–PLO forces on the defensive militarily, looking for a way to prevent their destruction. (On the eve of the Arab League meeting that called for the cease-fire, Syrian armor was deployed above the regional headquarters of the National Movement and the PLO.) At the same time, Syria in effect held in its hands the fate of the Christians, who were dependent on Syrian military strength. A decision in Damascus to accept the cease-fire, therefore, was virtually decisive for the Christians. As the two major players, Syria and the PLO could, if they agreed, largely control the game. The Arab League cease-fire took effect on October 18, and the Syrian forces, to be augmented by small contingents from the other Arab states, became the Arab Deterrent Force, which was ostensibly engaged in a peacekeeping operation.

Israeli Invasions. Everywhere but in the south the conflict settled into a stalemate, marked by continued violence but not much movement. In the south, the Israeli-Palestinian war became progressively more intense. It developed into the dominant dimension of the Lebanese conflict, overwhelming with its violence the continuing struggle among domestic Lebanese factions. Israeli policy under the Likud government elected in 1977 became more assertive in opposing the Palestinians and supporting the Christians in Lebanon. The first major Israeli invasion, in March 1978, seemed still to be a limited operation directed solely against the PLO. Israel's 25,000 troops stayed well clear of Syrian forces to the north and withdrew promptly under heavy US and UN pressure. Three years later, however, in April 1981, Israel raised the ante again and intervened militarily directly against the Syrian forces and in support of the Lebanese Christians. Israeli aircraft shot down two Syrian helicopters that were firing on Maronite forces on the ground. The Syrians raised their own stakes to match the Israelis, moving SAM antiaircraft missile batteries into Lebanon and keeping them there despite Israeli threats.

Finally, in June 1982, Israel acted to realize a fully developed and ambitious set of policy objectives in Lebanon, including the destruction of the PLO in Beirut, control over Lebanon by a Maronite government under Israeli aegis and linked by treaty with Israel, and Israeli hegemony over southern Lebanon. This time Israeli invading forces quickly engaged Syrian air and ground forces in Lebanon. The primary purpose seemed to be the neutralization of Syria as a military factor able to threaten the achievement of Israel's goals. Even in these circumstances, both sides seemed desirous of avoiding all-out war between them. Israel stopped short of engaging and defeating Syria's main forces in Lebanon or of driving them out of the country, and Syria swallowed its losses and refrained from mounting a serious military challenge to Israel's attack on Beirut.

If Israel's massive escalation of the conflict did not lead to war with Syria, it did leave the Lebanese civil war much changed. Following the Israeli pullback from central Lebanon, the war there reverted to a largely domestic conflict. The major Palestinian forces, long one of the three major external elements, were gone. Another of the three, the Israelis, having failed to achieve the internal Lebanese political outcome they desired but having rooted out the PLO, no longer played a direct and active role in the internal struggle. Only the Syrians were left, and their part was primarily political, albeit with substantial military clout still at hand. Israel's conflict was in the south, but it was largely with Lebanese opponents, sparked by the Shiites, who were resisting what they saw as foreign occupation.

Attempts to Manage the Conflict

During the pre–civil war years, in which Lebanon's political system unraveled and explosive tensions built up among Lebanese groupings and the Palestinians, there were no serious efforts by outside governments or organizations to stop the drift toward conflict. Quite the contrary.

As we have seen, such interest as was taken in the situation focused on improving the position of one or another faction that reflected the interests of the respective foreign governments. This was true for Syria as well as for other governments. Certainly, Israeli activities only increased the tension and the polarization. True, Nasser helped negotiate the Cairo Agreement of 1969 regulating PLO activities in Lebanon, but this was a poultice that did not get at the basic problems and certainly did not decrease the potential for involvement with Israel. Even during the first months of the war this continued to be the case. After all, civil strife had been endemic in Lebanon for many years, and other governments in the region did not feel threatened by it. The great powers had much the same attitude.

Syrian Political Intervention

By September 1975, however, the Syrians were worried. Violence was rampant, and the threat of partition was implicit in the situation. Damascus made its first move on September 20 when Foreign Minister Abdul Halim Khaddam worked out a cease-fire. As with so many subsequent cease-fires, this one lasted only briefly, Syria being unable to budge the local leaders enough to begin a process of political reconciliation. The Maronite Phalange, in fact, called for Arab League intervention, in part at least to outflank or to forestall Syrian efforts. During the following month, the Vatican and the government of France, the latter through former Prime Minister Couve de Murville, entered the picture briefly to urge greater cooperation between the Maronite President and the Sunni Moslem Prime Minister.

Syria persisted in its efforts to negotiate reforms in the distribution of power in Lebanon. By January 22, 1976, a new cease-fire was arranged. What was more important, agreement was announced on the framework of a political solution. A Syrian-Lebanese-Palestinian Higher Military Committee was to be formed to enforce the cease-fire. A month later, on February 14, a seventeen-point program of political reform, which became known as the "Constitutional Document," was announced. This effort, too, failed. The Christians, whose military position had deteriorated and who faced defeat, accepted it. Jumblat's National Movement, however, felt itself to be in a strong position and saw no reason to compromise on plans that did not, in its eyes, go nearly far enough.

Syria tightened the screws, beginning to put pressure on the Moslem left. Becoming ever more deeply involved in Lebanese politics with the decision that the Lebanese President must be replaced if reform was to succeed, Damascus also upped the ante militarily. In April, Syrian armored troops moved a short distance into Lebanon, and the ports of the National Movement were subjected to naval blockade. Under such pressure, a new cease-fire was arranged, and the Lebanese parliament met to adopt a constitutional amendment permitting an early election of a new president. In a few weeks, on May 8, under the protection of Syrian PLA units and Saiqa forces, the man generally assumed to be the Syrian candidate, Elias Sarkis, was elected.

Sarkis' election did not have the desired effect of providing new impetus for political reform. Tension increased between Syria and the PLO in Lebanon—it was during this period that Arafat began to mend his fences with Cairo. This latter development sparked a curious diplomatic intervention by the Libyan Prime Minister, who came to Beirut to negotiate a rapprochement between Syria and the Palestinians. The spectacle of a thaw in PLO-Egyptian relations so soon after the second withdrawal agreement between Israel and Egypt (Sinai II) was troubling for Tripoli, to say the least. But nothing availed, and Syria had arrived at the point where it had the choice of letting the conflict rage on or putting in enough force to control it. As we have seen, Assad took the latter course by sending a large Syrian force across the border on June 1. He was obviously determined to make whatever commitment was necessary to bring the conflict to a resolution he could live with.

Response to the Syrian Invasion

The possibility of a large-scale Syrian intervention had been of concern in a number of capitals for months. Prime Minister Yitzhak Rabin and Defense Minister Shimon Peres of Israel both warned publicly against such a move on January 8, 1976, Peres adding that if it occurred, Israel would "have to consider taking steps."[5] On the same day, a State Department spokesman in Washington announced that the United States was "opposed to any outside intervention in Lebanon, by any country, including Syria and Israel."[6] This remained the US position, although Washington approved and supported the efforts the Syrians had made to negotiate an end to the conflict. The United States had begun to focus on the Lebanese war at a high level only at the end of 1975. There were a number of reasons for this, but chief among them was the perception until then that the war did not threaten US interests. By early 1976, however, especially as Assad became more heavily involved, two possibilities began to worry Secretary of State Henry A. Kissinger. One was that the civil war would trigger an Arab-Israeli war and thus scuttle his hopes that after the 1976 US election year, his successful Middle East peace process could pick up again, in the first instance with Syria. Secondly, Kissinger was concerned that Assad might become so discredited by lack of success in Lebanon, as he staked more and more on his commitment there, that he could not resume the risky path of negotiation with Israel.

When word of the Syrian troop movement was received in Washington on the night of June 1, the United States decided, after some initial hesitation, that the intervention might be for the best so long as confrontation with Israel could be avoided. During the next few weeks the United States devoted itself, in effect, to preventing a dangerous escalation of the war by keeping Israel out of it. The Syrians were evidently anxious to avoid an expanded conflict. Indeed, one of their motives in trying to control the Lebanese situation was to forestall confrontation with Israel. The Israelis saw advantages in the Syrian move so long as it did not directly impinge on the security of their northern border. They gradually developed for the United States a definition of their limits in this respect, and Washington conveyed it to the Syrians. The Israelis termed their limits a "red line," widely misinterpreted in the press as consisting only of a line on a map. In Rabin's words, "The red line was an integrated complex of data and conditions, including the aim of the foreign forces operating in Lebanon and the target against which they are operating; their geographical position and its proximity to Israel; their military strength; and the length of time they spend in a given area."[7]

Arab League Cease-fire

Faced with the Syrian move, which disturbed the Egyptians in particular, Arab foreign ministers met in Cairo and agreed on June 9 to send an Arab peacekeeping force to Lebanon to supervise a cease-fire and take over from the Syrians. Some Arab units did in fact make it to Lebanon, but the League's mandate was indefinite enough that Syrian forces were able to operate essentially without interference. The Arab League could not be effective in calling for a cease-fire, however, until the principal players in Lebanon were prepared at least to acquiesce in a League decision. In addition to the Lebanese and Syrian governments and the PLO, Egypt had to be involved, given the spoiling role it could play, not least as an alternative—to Syria—source of support for the PLO. Only in the fall, after several more months of fighting, did this rare constellation of agreement occur. The October Arab League decision on a cease-fire, on a process of political reconciliation among Lebanese factions, and on an Arab peacekeeping force based on the Syrian troops was possible because both Syria and Egypt had become concerned enough about the Lebanese situation to put aside their regional rivalry for the moment at least.

The Arab League action was important. It brought an end to a year and a half of carnage, and it was some time before violence on the same scale occurred again. The decision was a one-time affair, however. The League made no attempt to interest itself on a continuing basis in Lebanon. Probably the only way for the League to maintain some degree of influence would have been through a genuinely multinational peace-keeping force commanded by an officer answerable to the League. But the peacekeeping force was actually a Syrian force, under the control of Assad and governed by Syrian policy concerns. There is a real question, moreover, whether the League had such a peacekeeping ca-pability in any case. The remarkable consensus achieved at the October meetings would in all likelihood have broken down. There was no staff or leadership in the League that could have used the force to accomplish political objectives related to Lebanon's domestic conflict, let alone cope with Israel and the Palestinians. The Arab League did not again play a major role in Lebanon, in part, presumably, because of the growing role assumed by Israel in the conflict after this point. When the need arose for a truly multilateral force to secure Israeli withdrawal in March 1978, it was the United Nations that provided it.

Enter the UN

The Israeli invasion of March 1978 raised the same specter of a Syrian-Israeli confrontation that had caused concern in Washington and elsewhere when the Syrians had invaded almost two years before. Again the United States took the lead in efforts to forestall such a possibility. Washington had a high stake in preventing the Middle East from exploding in expanded conflict. Negotiations leading to Camp David were then under way. With a UN Security Council meeting called at the formal behest of Lebanon, the United States proposed and obtained Council approval of a resolution calling for Israeli withdrawal and a UN peace-keeping force—the United Nations Interim Force in Lebanon (UNIFIL)—to confirm that withdrawal and to assist the Lebanese government in reestablishing its authority in southern Lebanon.

Until the creation of UNIFIL, the United Nations had played only a small role in the Lebanese conflict. UN Secretary General Kurt Waldheim issued an appeal to the parties on October 11, 1975, but no action by the Security Council was involved. The Council did meet on December 8 to consider the complaint of Lebanon about Israeli air attacks that took place on December 2; the United States ultimately vetoed a resolution condemning Israel. On March 30, 1976, following further generalized appeals, Waldheim called to the attention of the Security Council "the gravity of the situation in Lebanon," which he saw might have "im-plications extending well beyond the boundaries of that country."[8] The Lebanese government discouraged Council action, however, arguing that the conflict was a domestic one. Among the contending parties, especially the Moslem left, there was a reluctance to see the problem "internationalized" at that time. Following the Syrian invasion in June, though, National Movement leader Jumblat, faced with heavy Syrian pressure, sent a letter to Waldheim calling on the United Nations to intervene. Lebanese Prime Minister Rashid Karami was still opposed to such an action, and Jumblat's letter had no official status and therefore no effect.

It is not difficult to understand why there had been so little use made of the United Nations prior to the 1978 Israeli invasion. Most of the central issues in the Lebanese conflict were not only domestic but constitutional, involving the relationships among economic and religious groups in the society. There was, in fact, nothing useful the United Nations could have done about them. Still, the Security Council is frequently called into session as part of competitive political maneuvering among states, not because it can be useful with respect to the dispute in question. It is difficult to convene such a session, however, if the states most directly concerned do not wish to do so. In this case, neither Lebanon nor Syria was likely to see any advantage, and both could see disadvantages, in opening these delicate issues to wide international debate and action among states, many of whom were playing mischievous roles in the conflict. Israel, of course, would have seen nothing but trouble in UN consideration of the problem at any stage.

Yet the Israeli invasion was an occasion well-suited to UN intervention. The Security Council would not be considering matters in contention among the domestic parties. The point at issue was an Israeli action apart from the civil conflict, an action that had its roots and its primary significance in the Israeli-Palestinian dispute. The Council would, furthermore, be acting to contain a conflict, to forestall further foreign military involvement, and to reduce the chances for regional confrontation and wider war. Not least, the Israeli invasion was one subject on which the otherwise contentious Arab governments could agree. Finally, there was available to the Council a course of action that seemed appropriate to the occasion and that was within the United Nations's demonstrated capability—the establishment of a peacekeeping force.

This is not to say that the situation in the south of Lebanon was an ideal context for a peacekeeping force. Security Council resolution 425, setting up the force, did not represent a commitment of cooperation by the fighting forces that were to be operative in the area, primarily the PLO and the Lebanese Christian group under Major Saad Haddad that was maintained by Israel. Even Israel, the sole UN member state with genuine authority in the region, had accepted the resolution only under US pressure and without any intention of cooperating with the UN force, in which it had no confidence. UNIFIL, therefore, did not operate under an umbrella of sovereign authorities agreeable to its operation and committed to support it. The situation was quite the contrary.

Under such circumstances, UNIFIL was unable to carry out its full mandate. Its establishment was a factor in obtaining Israel's withdrawal, and it was able to confirm that withdrawal. It could not, however, fully restore international peace and security and assist the government of Lebanon in ensuring the return of its effective authority in the area, which resolution 425 called on it to do. It was able to maintain a buffer zone between the PLO-dominated area north of the Litani River and the Israeli-sponsored Haddad forces in a strip along the southern border. As with everything else in Lebanon, the situation was not so clear-cut, although broadly seen this was the position of UNIFIL. The Palestinians had posts within the UNIFIL area, however, and UNIFIL's headquarters were within the Haddad strip. The presence of the UN force no doubt reduced the violence between Haddad's men and the PLO, both of which groups would otherwise have tended to expand into the intervening territory, with resulting clashes. That it could not assist effectively in restoring Lebanese government authority was due primarily to the inability of the Lebanese to create a viable force for the purpose but also to the determination of Haddad to prevent its doing so.

US Political Intervention

While in 1978 the United States turned to the United Nations to help it get the Israelis out of Lebanon, three years later it acted unilaterally when an Israeli-Syrian confrontation threatened to touch off a regional conflict. This was the most major and most overt political commitment Washington had yet made in the six-year-old Lebanese conflict. It proved to be the beginning of an engagement that deepened over the next three years. The specific event that brought it about was the introduction into Lebanon of the Syrian antiaircraft missiles following the shooting down of two Syrian helicopters by Israeli aircraft in April 1981. Israeli threats to destroy the missiles seemed to have set the stage for the Israeli-Syrian conflict that had been brewing since 1978. Retired US diplomat Philip Habib was sent to the Middle East as President Ronald Reagan's Special Emissary. He persuaded the Israelis to refrain from attacking the missile sites while he attempted to negotiate a political solution.

He was shortly overtaken in this effort by the heavy Israeli bombing of Beirut on July 17, the result of an escalating flare-up of Israeli-PLO violence. A cease-fire was eventually arranged between Israel and the PLO. Here again, as in 1978, the United States found the United Nations to have useful attributes. Since neither the United States nor Israel would negotiate with the PLO, the US administration dealt with the Israelis through Habib and the United Nations dealt with the PLO through UNIFIL commander William Callaghan.

In both the "missile crisis" and the July cease-fire, the American intervention was focused on forestalling or ending conflict among external actors in the continuing Lebanese war. The United States did not become involved in the domestic issues as such. This had been the case as well during the informal US exercise of good offices between Syria and Israel in June-July 1976 and in the US use of the Security Council in March 1978. The next phase of US involvement followed the same pattern initially—in this case an effort to prevent an ultimate showdown between the Israelis and the PLO in Beirut. But largely because Israel had this time thrust so deeply into the heart of the domestic dispute, the United States found itself, at last, caught up in that as well. It was a costly departure for American policy.

Multinational Forces

Habib reentered the scene on June 7, 1982, in the wake of Israel's massive invasion. The Security Council had already, on June 6, called for a cease-fire and the withdrawal of Israeli troops, but Israel continued to advance on Beirut. By the end of the month, as Israel completed its encirclement of the Lebanese capital, the main issue for the US mediatory effort became the fate of the Palestinian forces in the city.

As arrangements were negotiated for their orderly departure, the question arose of a peacekeeping force to facilitate the operation. Israel rejected proposals for a UN force. Habib then worked out the establishment of a force composed of troops from three North Atlantic Treaty Organization countries, the United States, France, and Italy. This ad hoc Multinational Force (MNF) barely constituted an identifiable single force, since the contingents were deployed under separate understandings between Lebanon and the respective national governments and since there was no command structure for the force as a whole. Each national contingent operated independently. The mission of the MNF was a limited one: to assist the Lebanese armed forces in assuring the departure of PLO personnel from Beirut under safe and orderly conditions in a manner that would "further the restoration of the sovereignty and authority of the government of Lebanon over the Beirut area." President Reagan informed the UN Secretary General, in writing, of the US agreement to the Lebanese government's request for an American contingent to serve as part of the force. The deployment of the US force was consistent with Articles 1 and 2 of the UN Charter, he said, and with Security Council resolutions 508 and 509, adopted at the outset of the Israeli invasion.

During negotiation of the agreement on the departure of the Palestinians, the United States applied to Israel some of the heaviest political pressure in the thirty-four-year-old relationship between the two countries. Both in personal telephone calls and by letter Reagan demanded at sensitive points in the negotiation that Prime Minister Menachem Begin halt the repeated and relentless pounding of Beirut that was at times in violation of cease-fires worked out by Habib and that threatened to derail Habib's efforts on the broader issues. On August 12, the White House went so far as to issue a statement reporting that the President had "expressed his outrage" in a telephone call to Begin. "He emphasized," the statement said, "that Israel's action [bombing and shelling in Beirut] halted Ambassador Habib's negotiations. . . ." In conducting his talks, Habib could count on the political weight of the United States to support his position. For the PLO and the Lebanese factions and government, the belief that the United States was the only government that could move Israel—the Arabs consistently overrated the capacity of the United States to influence Israeli actions, but the Israelis were to some degree sensitive to US wishes—gave Habib authority he could not otherwise have had. His most crucial role, in fact, was probably the connection with Israel. He was one of many players on the Arab side of the negotiation, but it was up to him, backed by Washington, to bring Israel to agreement.

The first MNF accomplished what it was primarily intended to do: get the Palestinian fighters out of Lebanon without serious incident. Many Lebanese had hoped it would play more of a role in assuring the security of Beirut and in retrospect argued that it should have stayed and prevented the slaughter of Palestinians in the Sabra and Shatila refugee camps. But the thirty-day limit built into the mandate of the force precluded any continuing security role, although it would in fact have permitted troops to stay through the dates on which the killings occurred in the camps.

The second Multinational Force (MNF II)—American, French, and Italian troops and later a small British contingent—was quite a different affair, and the difference was instructive. Deployed hurriedly in the aftermath of the Palestinian killings, it sprang largely from a perceived psychological need to act, rather than from a clearly delineated task to be executed. More important, its mandate linked its role directly to the domestic conflict in Lebanon. To assist the Lebanese government in restoring "sovereignty and authority over the Beirut area" meant becoming involved in a civil conflict that had not been resolved. The military victory of the Maronite Phalange and the election of the Phalange chieftain as President under the aegis of Israeli military force did not settle the question of the distribution of political power that was at the heart of the internal struggle. Furthermore, the mandate of the MNF was extraordinarily vague and lacked criteria for determining when the mission had been completed.

A fundamental danger and weakness in the concept of the force lay in a perception gap between the Americans and the Lebanese (and other Arabs) as to the meaning of the American MNF contingent. Washington apparently recognized that providing the troops was a symbol of a certain level of US commitment to Lebanon's future. But to many in Lebanon and elsewhere in the Arab world it signaled an American undertaking to see that the Lebanese civil conflict was finally and satisfactorily settled. If the United States had fully understood the implications of this role and had had a strategy equal to it, the presence of the MNF could have been an important asset. What had apparently looked to Washington like a problem of establishing governmental authority turned out to be a struggle between Israel and its Lebanese proxies on the one hand and Syria and its proxies on the other. The issue was not only an internal political solution but also the future orientation of Lebanon relative to the competing regional powers on its borders, which were both still occupying sizable portions of its territory.

In retrospect, the much-debated question as to whether a multinational force or a multilateral, presumably UN, force was more appropriate seems largely moot. The situation in Lebanon in the wake of the Israeli invasion was so unstable and dynamic that the country was not yet ready for a "peacekeeping" type of force. In terms of third-party intervention, it was still more the Congo than the Sinai.[9] Theoretically, at least, a UN force would have avoided some of the worst problems of the MNF. It would not likely have been introduced with a mandate that had such political implications, since the Syrians would have been able to prevent it—through the Soviets if in no other way. Given that a UN force would necessarily have had the acquiescence of the most important players, it could have maintained a more neutral stance and avoided the heavy casualties suffered by the MNF. It would not have become part of the conflict, as the US forces did. What could it usefully have done, however, as the struggle between the Israeli-backed and Syrian-backed factions played itself out? Theoretically, again, an advantage of a national or multinational force was that it could play a forceful role in a situation not yet ready for a more passive one. But a force large enough to impose on the country, and on Syria, Gemayel's rule and his withdrawal agreement with Israel would have had to be very large and prepared to fight. Such a force was clearly not in the cards.

Conclusions

The interplay between domestic and external forces has been decisive for the character of the Lebanese conflict. It has been complex, dynamic, and pervasive, and it defies simple generalization. A number of useful comments can be made, however, about the process of escalation and about the effects of outside efforts to resolve or to manage the conflict, although these comments are subject to many caveats.

• Escalation of the Lebanese civil war has sprung not primarily from the domestic power struggle within the country but from the triangular relationship of three non-Lebanese actors—Syria, Israel, and the PLO. True, the Lebanese domestic factions all have had their foreign supporters, and a number of states have played out regional rivalries on the Lebanese stage. But the outside powers were not drawn into serious conflict simply by their support of opposing domestic factions. The broader warfare that became a subject of worldwide concern occurred because the Israeli-Palestinian conflict was ultimately fought out in a Lebanese context and because Syria and Israel saw their vital interests involved in the outcome of the domestic civil war.

• There are a number of reasons why escalation has stopped short of an all-out Syrian-Israeli war. Throughout most of the period, neither side saw such a war as necessary or even helpful to the achievement of its goals in Lebanon. One of the reasons Syria has wanted to bring the Lebanese turmoil under control, in fact, is precisely so that the civil war would not lead to conflict with Israel. When Israel invaded in 1982 to destroy the PLO and to shape a favorable Lebanese political outcome, it took the Syrians out of play only incidentally to pursuing these main goals. By the time it had failed to impose its political solution and had seen Syria as an obstacle to its success, the Israeli public was in no mood for military confrontation with Syria. Israel fell back on other means to secure its minimum goals in Lebanon.

• Escalation to a superpower conflict has probably not been a serious risk at any time. Washington foolishly but briefly tried to justify its military presence in Lebanon in 1982–83 as a barrier to Soviet expansion, but neither power has seen Lebanon as vital to its interests. The most likely route to their involvement would have been through a serious Syrian-Israeli war, but this has not occurred.

• Interventions to resolve or to manage the conflict have had least success in attempting to settle the basic domestic political problem. The most nearly successful of such attempts has been a unilateral national effort—the combination of persistent diplomacy and military force by the Syrians. But beyond that, outside mediation without muscle has seemed of limited value.

• Attempts by governments and organizations to bring a halt to hostilities, without necessarily affecting the underlying issues, have been more successful, though only temporarily so. Here again, diplomacy with some clout behind it has been the most effective in difficult circumstances. Syrian force helped create the conditions that made possible the cease-fire arranged by the Arab League in October 1976. This cease-fire demonstrated an important contribution that multilateral organizations can make in such cases, even where a single state is making the running. They can bring together in support of a cease-fire or other initiative outside governments that might otherwise, through their backing of contending factions, make it possible for those factions to frustrate the initiative in question. The important cease-fires arranged by Ambassador Habib in July 1981 and at various stages in 1982 were doubtless due in part to the political weight of the United States, especially with Israel.

• A third category of intervention has been devoted entirely to forestalling the entry of additional players into the hostilities or to inducing their withdrawal. Attempts to resolve the conflict and to halt hostilities have also been undertaken partly, at times primarily, in order to prevent the spread of the conflict. The most notable examples involved Israel and were undertaken principally by the United States. American good offices at the time of the 1976 Syrian invasion required confidentiality and the confidence of Syria and Israel, which the United States at that time enjoyed. It could not have been done by an organization, though a UN official who was highly regarded personally could theoretically have done it. Israel had no such regard for any UN-connected diplomat, however. Securing the withdrawal of Israel in 1978 was also mainly a US initiative, but was a good example of the utility of the United Nations in facilitating an operation undertaken basically by a national government—in this case by creating UNIFIL. Finally, the prolonged effort to bring about conditions that would lead to Israel's withdrawal in 1982–83 involved many players, but again the United States played the major role. The relative isolation of Israel from other contacts made any other approach impractical.

• The United Nations and the Arab League had specific and serious limitations in dealing with the Lebanese problem. In its early phases, the domestic issues predominated and were difficult for a multilateral organization to treat. In the later phases, Israel became a major player and neither organization could deal very effectively, the League not at all, with the Israelis.

• The United Nations suffered also from a lack of clout behind its decisions. Unless influential member states are prepared to put their individual weight behind Security Council actions, there is little to induce unwilling states to accede. This member states have seldom been willing to do, as in the Council's calls for a cease-fire in the Israeli invasion of 1982. It must be said, however, that the UN resolutions at times seemed to be fired off into the blue, at a time and in circumstances when no effective result could have been expected regardless of follow-up by member states. It is a truism that UN actions can be most effective when they reflect the genuine determination of a major power or powers to bring about a certain result. Security Council efforts to end the 1978 Israeli invasion are a case in point, since the United States used the United Nations at that time to help it bring about this result. But in most cases little integration seems to be achieved between the rhythm and motivation of UN actions and the practical realities and demands of interstate relations that actually determine the outcomes.

• At no time has Lebanon been a good setting for the standard form of peacekeeping. Syrian forces imposed themselves on the situation, somewhat as the United Nations had done earlier in the Congo, and had some success in establishing a certain balance. But they became embroiled in the conflict eventually and lost their authority. Operations without effective combat forces, such as UNIFIL and the second Multinational Force in 1982–83, suffered from two limiting factors: a minimally stable status quo did not exist, and not all the parties were prepared to cooperate. UNIFIL did remarkably well under such circumstances, but it is doubtful that the attempt would have been justifiable on peacekeeping grounds alone—that is, leaving aside the desirability of inducing Israeli forces to withdraw.

• The essentially national forces of the second Multinational Force, sent in as the Israelis withdrew from Beirut, encountered the same problem but suffered also from a faulty mandate. In the conditions then existing, they had a partisan mission without anything like the force needed to carry it out, if indeed that was possible or desirable under any circumstances. A multilateral force, presumably under UN aegis, with a standard peacekeeping mandate, might have played a valuable role in the wake of the Israeli withdrawal. It is questionable whether it should have been introduced, given the turbulence still prevailing, but it would have been far more likely to stick to, and to perform, a useful function than the national contingents, the American force in particular.

• The question arises whether these lessons from the Lebanese experience can be applied more widely. Some of them probably can be. It is likely to be generally true that external interventions will have greater success in halting hostilities and preventing the spread of conflict than they will have in resolving disputes. A more complex question is the utility of various kinds of interventionist forces. Intervention by national forces, by ad hoc groupings of national forces or by forces under the aegis of established multilateral organizations all seem to have advantages and disadvantages that can be widely applied. Each can be used to good effect in different situations. The circumstances in which they are to be used determine the type of force likely to be successful. The principal questions to be asked are: is military clout required, is the situation under the control of parties supportive of the intervention, and which sponsorship and force composition are acceptable to the parties. If the use of military force, or the threat of its use, is a necessary ingredient, only national units or ad hoc groups of national units will suffice. The use of Syrian forces in June 1976 is an example. They can be at least partly legitimized by a multilateral organization, as Syria's force was several months after it was introduced, but the operation is still essentially national.

In situations not requiring the use of force, a multilateral operation has important advantages. It has established procedures that generally keep it from becoming entangled in the conflict. Its introduction and mandate must be approved by the broadly representative UN Security Council, and it is thus unlikely to go into situations where it will be a partisan factor. Its use promotes the rule of law and the strength of international institutions. It normally would also be politically more neutral than a national force, but here is the rub in Lebanon. Neutrality is in the eye of the beholder, in this case the parties to the dispute. A characteristic of the Lebanese conflict has seemed to be that a true neutral, in the perception of all the parties, does not exist. To Israel no multilateral force, either of the United Nations or *a fortiori* of the Arab League, is neutral. With respect to the United Nations, misuse of the organization by a third world majority intent on pushing its own causes has been largely responsible for damaging its credibility and legitimacy as a neutral force. A force that included US troops, however acceptable to Israel, was suspect in Syrian and some Lebanese eyes. And so forth. There may be a need for a peacekeeping force with a new mandate in Lebanon—for example, if Syrian and Israeli troops pull out—and it will be important to deal imaginatively with this problem of acceptance.

• The foregoing paragraph assumes that a UN force cannot be expected to carry out a mission requiring outright combat, especially in a domestic dispute. It assumes, in short, that the Congo model cannot be repeated today. This is almost certainly true, but in looking into the future it might be useful to ask whether we should be content with that situation. Or, should there be an effort to build support for the principle of UN intervention in internal conflicts that threaten international peace or that are in themselves highly destructive of lives and human rights—intervention that might include the use of force?

• Escalation and intervention are ambiguous and interlocked concepts. In Lebanon, major escalation has generally come through the intervention of non-Lebanese players, beginning with the full-scale entry of the PLO into the fighting in early 1976. In turn, escalation, with the possibility of more to come, has brought the concerned diplomatic interventions of influential states and international organizations trying to limit or to resolve the conflict. Escalation has brought changes in the character of the war that sometimes have made the conflict easier to deal with politically. It remains to be seen whether the major Israeli intervention and escalation of 1982–83 has produced a domestic situation that will be possible to stabilize.

Notes

1. Jonathan Randall, *Going All the Way* (New York: Random House, 1984), p. 57.

2. The National Pact was an unwritten agreement by which the Lebanese Moslems gave up their aim of union with the Arab world in exchange for renunciation by the Christians of protection by the West, principally France. It included a distribution of the main governmental offices in such a way as to reflect the approximate size of the various religious groups in the population of the country. The president was to be a Maronite Christian, for example, and the prime minister a Sunni Moslem. The distribution of seats in the legislature was six to five in favor of the Christians.

3. *Events* (London, February 11, 1977). Quoted by Charles E. Waterman in "Lebanon's Continuing Crisis," *Current History* (January 1978), p. 19.

4. *The New York Times*, September 13, 1975, and October 5, 1975. Quoted by Norman Howard in "Upheaval in Lebanon," *Current History* (January 1976), p. 36.

5. Peres interview with *Maariv*, quoted in *Arab Report & Record*, Issue I (January 1–15, 1976), p. 30.

6. Ibid.

7. Statement to Knesset, June 13, 1976. *Arab Report & Record*, Issue II (June 1–15, 1976), p. 371.

8. *United Nations Chronicle*, Vol. XIII, No. 4 (April 1976), p. 28.

9. In 1960–61 a UN force of more than 20,000 troops from eighteen countries, including a small combat air force, engaged in active military operations in the newly independent Congo to help maintain the territorial integrity and political independence of the country and to assist the central government in restoring and maintaining law and order. The force—United Nations Operations in the Congo (ONUC)—was acting under a Security Council resolution of July 14, 1960, authorizing the Secretary General to provide the government with "such military assistance as may be necessary" to enable its own security forces to carry out their tasks. As the operation developed, it was bitterly opposed by the Soviet Union.

PART TWO

Interstate Conflicts

III

The Iran-Iraq War

Barry Rubin

The Iran-Iraq war may be the bloodiest international conflict since World War II. Resistant to all negotiating efforts since its start in September–October 1980, the conflict has posed unique challenges to would-be mediators and tremendous threats to regional stability.

Underlying the war are long-standing enmities and disputes: friction between Arabs and Persians and between Sunni and Shia Moslems, disagreements over the boundary line in the Shatt al-Arab waterway, and conflicting political systems and different international orientations during the era of the Shah of Iran. These issues led to a "cold war" between the two countries that ended with the Algiers agreement of 1975, in which they pledged mutual non-subversion and a settlement of the frontier dispute.

This accord, and the period of peace it brought, fell apart in the aftermath of the Iranian revolution. When the Shah was driven from his throne and an Islamic regime came into power in February 1979, the regional political and power balance seemed essentially altered. In Tehran there was a new order under the leadership of Ayatollah Ruhollah Khomeini, which seemed to be both militarily weaker and politically more threatening than its predecessor. The Islamic republic began to propagandize for the overthrow of other Persian Gulf regimes, while purging the Iranian Army. In November 1979, Iranian students, with support from Khomeini, took over the US Embassy in Iran and held American diplomats as hostages, sparking a crisis that ended only in January 1981.

Barry Rubin is a fellow at the Foreign Policy Institute of the Johns Hopkins School of Advanced International Studies. His books include *Secrets of State: The State Department and the Struggle Over US Foreign Policy* (New York: Oxford University Press, 1985); *Paved With Good Intentions: The American Experience and Iran* (New York: Oxford University Press, 1980); and *The Arab States and the Palestine Conflict* (Syracuse: Syracuse University Press, 1982).

Motives for the War

There has been much debate among specialists and policy analysts about Iraq's motives in invading Iran. As in other cases, most notably the Soviet invasion of Afghanistan, the factors behind Baghdad's action can be divided into "offensive" and "defensive" calculations. Since both kinds of considerations were involved, it is pointless to try to determine which was primary.

On the "offensive" side of the ledger, the political turmoil in Iran and the apparent gutting of the Iranian military seemed to create a tremendous opportunity for Iraq. To defeat Tehran, and even to bring down Khomeini's regime, seemed a relatively easy task to Baghdad's rulers. Iraq would then emerge as the most powerful state in the Gulf— with oil-rich and wealthy countries on all its shores—and as the protector of the Arab world. There was also an opportunity to dispose of the 1975 Algiers agreement, which Baghdad saw as a necessary concession from weakness.

These were the thoughts that led Iraq to be confident enough to launch an offensive. Its decision to attack sprang also from deep concerns and a sense of threat. Many Moslems responded enthusiastically to Khomeini's revolution. Iraq, as a relatively secular regime with predominant power in the hands of a Sunni minority, would be a tempting target for Iran, which could help the Shia majority in Iraq stage an Islamic fundamentalist revolution. In fact, there is evidence of Iranian assistance to such groups in Iraq, just as Baghdad aided dissidents among Iran's Arab minority.

These two sets of factors were mutually reinforcing in seeming to urge immediate action. At the same time, Iraq's motives indicate that this was not to be a war over territory or, for that matter, over any simple definable material issues. Rather, it was to be a war for supremacy and survival by two totalitarian regimes that were relatively indifferent to casualties. On another level, it was a battle between two governmental and ideological systems—radical Arab nationalism and Islamic fundamentalism—that could end only with the collapse of one of them or in mutual exhaustion. Obviously, these circumstances made any mediation or solution much more difficult.

Four Phases of the Conflict

The war passed through four distinct phases in its first four years: the original, seemingly triumphant Iraqi offensive; Iran's comeback in clearing Iraqi forces off its soil; Iran's penetration into Iraq and the series of "final offensives"; and the Iraqi-initiated "war of the tankers" against Gulf shipping.

1. Iraqi offensive. Iraq's armies crossed into Iran in September 1980 and quickly drove back the defenders, capturing key cities. Iran did not collapse but rallied in a war of national defense. The Iranian Army, supplemented by determined pro-regime volunteers, finally held. Iraqi strategy was also flawed in lacking clear objectives and in following an excessively cautious plan. By the spring of 1981, Baghdad's advance had been halted and the Iraqi leaders had no idea how to bring the war to an end.

To avoid reprisals, both sides limited attacks on each other's oil facilities. True, Iran's Abadan refinery was destroyed and production fell until adjustments could be made, but many tempting targets—including pipelines and storage tanks—remained untouched. Iraq, however, faced more serious problems, since Iran's naval control of the upper Gulf blocked Iraqi exports by sea, while Iran's ally, Syria, closed Iraq's pipeline to the Mediterranean Sea.

2. Iranian counteroffensives. Highly motivated, imaginative, and willing to take heavy losses, the Iranians now waged counteroffensives in the war's second phase. Although still internationally isolated, Tehran received badly needed billions of dollars in assets from the settlement of the hostage crisis. The Iraqi troops were not eager to die to hold foreign territory that their government had no intention of keeping. In dramatic battles in which they suffered large numbers of prisoners, Baghdad's armies were pushed back to the border by the summer of 1982.

Iran's leaders now faced a major decision. Should they seek to end the war on a territorial basis, or should their aim be to advance toward Iraq's main cities and topple the Baghdad government? Although some military officers apparently suggested the former option, Khomeini and the political decision makers did not hesitate to choose the latter. On July 14, 1982, Iranian troops crossed over into Iraq.

3. Iranian "final offensives." This move initiated the war's third phase. Whereas formerly Iraq was on top in the battle, now Iran seemed the likely victor. Such an analysis, however, left out all-important psychological and tactical matters. Iraqi troops were now well-entrenched and protecting their own soil. Iranian human-wave assaults, a tactic that had worked well against demoralized Iraqi forces on Iranian territory, failed, with heavy losses on the Iraqi side of the border.

Tehran, however, was not discouraged. In addition to a belief that one more push might bring a breakthrough, there was a calculation that Iran was on the winning end of a war of attrition. It was exporting over two million barrels of oil a day, while money-starved Iraq sold less than one-third that amount. Baghdad was dependent on grants from Arab allies and on being able to put off its creditors. It was only a matter of time, Iranian leaders believed, until Iraq would collapse.

4. Tanker war. Baghdad, too, was aware of this situation, which led to the war's fourth phase in the autumn of 1983. Iraq decided to strike against tankers carrying Iran's oil. By damaging Tehran's economy and by eliminating its financial attritional advantage, Iraq thought it could provide Iran with a new incentive to end the war. Meanwhile, Baghdad found enough loans—plus planned construction of new oil pipelines—to keep up its own morale. But as it turned out, Iraq could not damage Iran's exports enough to injure its rival seriously.

The war was escalated during this fourth phase when Iraq used some of its new military equipment, particularly French-built Super Etandard fighter-bombers, to attack Iranian oil installations. This strategy was designed not only to damage Iran's oil exports, and hence the Iranian economy, but also to raise the conflict's stakes to create a greater incentive for the international community and the superpowers to aid Iraq and to bring the war to an end.

Ironically, Iraq was escalating the war to force an Iranian counter-escalation in such a way as to bring additional international forces into line against Tehran. By attacking shipping on its way to Iran's Khargh island, Baghdad created a situation that threatened the vital flow of oil out of the Gulf. If Iran attacked tankers from Saudi Arabia, Kuwait, and the United Arab Emirates, Iraq would benefit further. Baghdad hoped that in response the West would seek to limit Iran's military supplies, cut purchases of Iranian oil, step up mediation efforts, and even take military action against Iran in order to protect the Gulf Arab countries and the shipping lanes.

The superpower ramifications of these developments will be considered below, but the effects on regional actors were quite considerable. As it turned out, Iran did counterattack by damaging several tankers shipping oil from Kuwait and Saudi Arabia. Nevertheless, Iran was restrained enough to avoid setting off a full-scale crisis, and it limited such actions. Iraq's own attacks on Iran had little effect, and they did not make the Iranians desperate enough to set off a chain of events—by trying to block the Straits leading out of the Gulf, for example—that might cause a global crisis. The international oil glut and the surplus of tankers for hire also prevented any disruption of energy markets.

Thus, while the tanker war heightened the danger and concern of the regional states, involving as it did a threat to their livelihood and the use of armed force against civilian shipping, the degree of escalation taking place was surprisingly limited. There were no direct attacks on the Arab states of the Gulf, no all-out attempts to overthrow them, and no serious interference with the great majority of Gulf shipping. As a war within a war, this phase was also open to mediation efforts even if the larger war continued.

The Iranians, of course, were eager to end the Iraqi attacks on their petroleum installations and on tankers picking up oil at these facilities. In exchange, they offered to cease their own sporadic attacks against ships carrying Saudi and Kuwaiti oil. In August 1984, Tehran actually made a unilateral pledge on this latter point, thanks in part to the UN Secretary General's efforts to limit damage to noncombatants. Iran's promise, however, was broken after a few weeks.

Iran's willingness to negotiate on the tanker attacks, though, was not a step toward diplomacy over the entire war. Tehran specifically excluded any willingness to allow a renewal of Iraqi oil exports through the Gulf. Without such a provision, Baghdad would never agree to any deal. Consequently, Iran's interest in such an exchange was fundamentally an attempt to use leverage to open a rift between the other Gulf Arab states and Iraq.

Effects on Neighboring States

Each phase of the war had a different effect on outside involvement and prospects for mediation. The war's effect on the other Gulf Arab states and on the United States and the Soviet Union should be considered separately. The other Arab states of the Gulf—Kuwait, Saudi Arabia, the United Arab Emirates, Bahrain, Qatar, and Oman—are all militarily weak, thinly populated monarchies, although the first three have considerable oil wealth. As Arab states, they are pro-Iraq; as conservative monarchies, they worry about Iranian republican and revolutionary subversion. Since their rulers and most of the people are Sunni Moslems, they are also inclined against the Shia Islam of Khomeini. They mistrust Baghdad as well, however, and cannot be enthusiastic, without reservation, about an Iraqi victory. Finally, given their weakness, wealth, fragile social fabric, and vulnerable oil installations, they would prefer to avoid any direct involvement in the fighting.

The Gulf monarchies have made some positive efforts to strengthen their security, including arms purchases and the formation of an alliance against external and internal radical forces—the Gulf Cooperation Council (GCC). The GCC was organized as a self-defense and an economic cooperation group. Its membership comprises all the Arab states of the Gulf other than Iraq. The exclusion of both Iran and Iraq evinced the founders' desire to stay out of the war and to limit dependence on the two states seeking regional dominance. The GCC announced its own rapid deployment force, shared intelligence, lowered customs and visa barriers, and also sought to coordinate economic development plans. In short, one effect of the war was to foster better relations and a resolution of differences among the threatened regional states. The most concrete result of this activity was Saudi Arabia's shooting down, with considerable US assistance, of an Iranian Phantom fighter in June 1984. This success discouraged Iranian attacks on shipping in Saudi waters.

During the first phase of the war, the other Gulf states welcomed Iraqi victories. As the tide began to turn, however, they became increasingly nervous and sought an end to the war in various ways, including making an offer to finance huge reparations to Iran. Tehran, though, demanded GCC pressure on Iraqi President Saddam Hussein to resign. While the Saudis might have explored this option, they lacked the leverage and the nerve to press for such an outcome. Clearly, so long as Iran's demand was for the overthrow of the Iraqi government, there was little the other regional states could do either to mediate or to facilitate an acceptable solution.

Since Iran was still conscious of some need to maintain correct relations with the GCC states, it was willing to work with them on secondary issues. The clearest example of such cooperation was the negotiation on cleaning up an oil leak from off-shore Iranian installations damaged by Iraq—a leak that was polluting Gulf waters. Active involvement by the GCC regimes helped persuade the Iranians to allow a technical team to cap the well. Large numbers of Iranians have also continued to take the Islamic pilgrimage to Mecca, Saudi Arabia, which has mutually agreed guidelines with Iran; however, the pilgrims have caused some problems for the Saudi authorities.

Special consideration should be given to the roles of two neighboring non-Arab states: Turkey and Pakistan. Both countries wish to maintain good relations with next-door Iran despite their opposition to Tehran's militant revolutionary fundamentalism. They also have strong ties to the Arab, and specifically the Iraqi, side, including very important trade relations. Their opposition to any expansion of Soviet influence or of regional instability are additional incentives for them to seek an end to the war. Both countries have tried to mediate at a high level, although their efforts have not been successful. Since they are perceived by both sides as neutral and friendly at the same time—and they are Islamic peoples, a plus for Iran—they remain good potential go-betweens.

US and Soviet Involvement

As one turns to US and Soviet involvement in the conflict, it is important to keep in mind that both Iran and Iraq, as well as the other Gulf states, share a cultural/ideological belief in superpower omnipresence and omnipotence. Each believes that superpower intervention, if exercised on its own behalf, could end the war immediately. The obverse of that is belief in superpower responsibility for the continuation of the war. There are significant barriers, however, to any acceptance of the United States or the Soviet Union as mediators.

The most obvious aspect of the problem is the deep and pervasive anti-Americanism of Iran's leadership and revolution. The upheaval against the Shah and the ensuing hostage crisis were based on a thorough-going rejection of US influence without ever resolving the belief of the Iranians in the extent of US power. Thus, Washington is seen as standing behind every domestic threat and foreign foe, most particularly as the mainstay of Iraq and of the "un-Islamic" Gulf monarchies. Needless to say, the United States has no significant leverage with Iran: Washington's support for any initiative is almost in itself sufficient to guarantee Tehran's opposition. The USSR's long border with Iran and Moscow's ability to benefit from any escalation of US-Iranian confrontation also inhibit US policy.

US-Iraqi relations are equally characterized by past mistrust. Baghdad's interest in dominating the Gulf Arab states, its ties with Moscow, its anti-American radicalism, and its extreme stand on the Arab-Israeli conflict provoked tension. In the first half of the 1970's, the United States sided with Iran against Iraq in supporting a Kurdish rebellion there. Given Iraq's overall posture, including its help for terrorism, Washington is unlikely to sell it arms. Abiding interests make formal neutrality and a limited tilt toward Iraq the proper policy.

US goals are defined as helping to protect the Gulf Arab monarchies and to halt the spread of radical fundamentalism, not to bring an Iraqi victory. This makes for an indirect, largely noninterventionist stand. Iraq, for its part, wants Washington to be even more partisan in its cause. There can be no productive mediation role for the United States, even—given Iran's sensitivities—a low profile or an indirect one.

At first, the USSR seems a more promising mediator and one that is not absolutely excluded, as is the United States. Nonetheless, while the opportunities of such a role are attractive for Moscow, its risks are less appealing. First of all, despite the deeply strained character of US-Iranian relations, an attempt by the USSR to dominate Iran would bring a severe US reaction, a response implied by the Carter Doctrine committing the United States to defense of the Gulf area from Soviet aggression. Frustrated in its attempts to improve relations with Iran, the Soviet Union now expects little to its advantage from the Islamic republic.

All along, Moscow's political line has been that the war is a mistake, distracting both sides from what should be their main objective: attacking the interests of the United States and its friends. Such an antiwar position has not been appealing to the Khomeini regime. After the pro-Soviet Iranian Tudeh (Communist) party opposed an Iranian advance onto Iraqi soil, it was systematically repressed. Iran has a long anti-Russian tradition; Islamic fundamentalists, moreover, are not enamored of communism. The Soviet invasion and occupation of Afghanistan has not helped matters.

While Iraq finds the Soviets more useful than Iran does, it trusts them no more. There is great bitterness in Baghdad over the USSR's abandonment of its alliance with Iraq during the war. While the Soviets are Iraq's main arms supplier—it should not be forgotten that Moscow is profiting greatly by the war—Baghdad is fiercely independent of Soviet influence. Its economic interests impel it toward the West.

For Moscow to make a determined effort at mediation, it must transcend the suspicions of both sides. Even so, it would risk further antagonizing one or both of them. Certainly, it lacks the leverage to broker an agreement. While a consolidated US-USSR peace effort sounds attractive in theory, international realities make it unlikely that such an effort will be undertaken. Besides, by combining forces the two superpowers would only compound the weaknesses of each as a mediator. If it is to be resolved at all, the Iran-Iraq war will require a relatively low-key and disinterested third party.

Potential for Further Escalation of the War

In spite of the strain of the tanker war—and the failure of this phase to escalate seriously may in fact have proved the point—the conflict is likely to remain bilateral. The war certainly has the potential for escalation to the highest level, since it involves vital oil supplies and reserves, key shipping routes, potential clashes between superpower interests, and strategically located territories. Neither Iran nor Iraq sees horizontal escalation in its interest, however, and the United States and the Soviet Union want to avoid involvement because they want to remain on the best possible terms with both Iran and Iraq—and with the GCC countries, which oppose direct superpower intervention. The Soviet Union is already tied down in Afghanistan, while the US government faces severe domestic constraints.

For Iraq, it is preferable to have the rest of the Gulf Arab countries act as a secure rear area and as a source of financial support. The Gulf monarchies would have little direct military effect given their own weakness, although Egyptian arms and Jordanian volunteers were solicited. At the same time, with Iraq's limited port facilities closed by the fighting, goods can be safely shipped through Kuwait or Saudi

Arabia. The Gulf monarchies have also supplied vast amounts of money—estimates range around the $30 billion mark—and have sold a million barrels of oil a day with the proceeds earmarked for Iraqi coffers.

Iran has had somewhat less interest in keeping the war limited. In ideological terms it finds the Gulf Arab monarchies as offensive as its enemy Iraq, with whom they are allied. Iranian propaganda and subversive activities have sought the overthrow of these regimes. Nevertheless, Tehran has limited such efforts and employed them more for the sake of leverage than for revolution. The main purpose of Iranian policy has been to frighten or to threaten those countries into stopping their aid to Iraq. Furthermore, Iran has had its hands full militarily in fighting Iraq and has no serious desire to open new fronts. Tehran is aware of its own limited resources, and despite its propaganda stance of fearlessness toward Washington, it is aware as well of US willingness to help the Gulf states if they are attacked.

While the war is therefore likely to remain limited to the two combatants, it is also likely to remain unresolved. The Iranian objective remains the annihilation of the Iraqi government. In fact, even if the war was to end, the two countries would probably remain in rivalry, both looking forward to a potential second round.

Prospects for Mediation

Prerequisites for successful mediation include: a basis for compromise that is both legitimate and possible, given the objectives of the sides involved; the acceptance by the two sides that no alternatives to negotiation are practicable; the existence of a mutually satisfactory mediator with the necessary backing from other parties; leverage on the part of those favoring a settlement; a stake in settling the conflict on the part of those directly involved as well as on the part of influential outsiders; and the formulation of acceptable solutions.

In the Iran-Iraq conflict, the material disputes between the parties are resolvable, technical ones. It is certainly possible, though not necessarily easy, to work out agreements about the relatively small pieces of mutually claimed border territory, the right of navigation on the Shatt al-Arab waterway that forms much of the boundary, pledges of non-interference in each other's internal affairs, and free navigation of the Gulf. Given the xenophobia of the two sides, they might prefer no foreign presence, or at most a limited number of observers, along the border rather than any truce force. Arriving at an amount for Iranian reparation claims will also be a contentious but resolvable problem.

The real issues are the questions of principle: two regimes that believe they cannot live side by side, and an Iran that thinks compromise is immoral and treasonous. In light of these attitudes, the current situation is not promising for a quick end to the war. It may point the way to an eventual solution, however. Iranian offensives have failed, with high casualties incurred, and the Iraqis are well-supplied and well-entrenched. It is hard to believe that an all-out attack can succeed, and this fact must be dawning on Iran's leadership.

If the dramatic-breakthrough option has failed, the war-of-attrition strategy also does not look promising for Iran. Iraq has been able to obtain credits from other countries to keep its economy going. Baghdad can hold on long enough to allow the construction of new petroleum pipelines that will permit a vast increase in its oil exports and, hence, in income. There are no signs of an internal revolt or coup against a regime willing to use all means of repression to stay in power.

While Iran's war-ending efforts have failed—leaving Tehran searching for a new strategy—Iraq's war against the tankers has succeeded only in small part. Iran's income has been cut but not severely damaged; the superpowers are helping Iraq more but are incapable of bringing it either peace or victory. Consequently, the war continues to be in an objective stalemate, although not necessarily in a subjective stalemate.

The Iranian leadership, resting on the indomitable will of Ayatollah Khomeini, continues to talk about demands ranging from the replacement of Iraq's Baathist government with an Islamic fundamentalist one to the mere replacement of Iraqi dictator Saddam Hussein and, presumably, his closest associates. This is a pretty narrow range from the standpoint of negotiations. Sometimes, other objectives are hinted at—a tribunal to find Iraq guilty of starting the war, large amounts of reparations—that more likely complement rather than displace the more extreme goals.

Even with Iran's mounting problems, however, the pressure is still heavy on Baghdad. Its economic problems are merely being postponed, and war weariness is greater than it is in Iran. There must be real temptation for officers to consider attempts to overthrow their own leaders, but Baghdad's intelligence is good and its repression is merciless. Actually, an Iranian peace initiative might pose a danger to Iraq, even though it avidly seeks a settlement, since Baghdad would then face the question of making major concessions. If Iraq will not lose, Iraq cannot win.

An end to the war will come only from changing conditions. In other words, mediation can spring in when the opportunity arises but probably cannot create such an opportunity. Such an opportunity might be presented by the death of either Khomeini or Saddam Hussein or a radical change in the government of either country. If Khomeini dies, Iran would undergo an internal jockeying for power that would not allow any quick shift in gears—anyone advocating peace would be accused by rivals of betraying Khomeini's ideology—but that could lead to an increasing flexibility on the issue. If Saddam Hussein was to die, or to be replaced, Iranians favoring a settlement could try to convince Khomeini that his bête noire was gone and therefore the vendetta could end. After all, a similar situation—the Shah's death—helped resolve the hostage crisis.

Certainly, there are trends toward mutual war weariness and exhaustion. These tendencies in themselves are insufficient, however, to effect change in two such tightly controlled dictatorships. If Iran's rulers concluded that continuation of the war might result in internal upheaval, they might be prompted to change course. Yet this is not happening now and is offset by other factors as well.

We are dealing here with two regimes and political cultures that see conflict and violence as natural and acceptable parts of international relations rather than as exceptional, even pathological, deviations from the norm. Each of them feels that showing weakness will lead only to even further losses of leverage and opportunity.

Meanwhile, those most immediately involved that want the war to end, the Gulf Arab states, are too weak and fearful to forward such an outcome. The Iraqis will punish any diminution of support with threats and terrorism; the Iranians will similarly reward any escalation of support for Baghdad. Tehran essentially considers the Gulf governments to be as illegitimate as that of Iraq but wants to split them away from supporting Iraqi President Saddam Hussein. Iraq sees them as endless financial reservoirs and as political hostages.

Unable to serve as mediators themselves, the GCC states would like to find some outside or international force to play this role. Ironically, they fear any growing influence for either superpower in the subregion yet at the same time would be only too happy to be rescued by a US and/or a Soviet deus ex machina that would bring the fighting to an end. As we have seen, this is not going to happen. The Gulf states could help any negotiating process by supplying funds for reparations but can exercise precious little influence.

Many other would-be mediators have stepped forward, perhaps more than in any other recent war. They include African leaders such as Guinea's late President Ahmed Sékou Touré, Swedish Prime Minister Olof Palme on behalf of the UN Secretary General, the Foreign Ministers of India, Japan, and Pakistan, PLO chief Yasir Arafat, the Islamic Conference Organization (ICO), the nonaligned movement, and UN officials. Initiatives were launched by Algeria in March and July 1982 and by Turkey in August 1982.

There are two interesting precedents for mediation here. One is the Algerian-brokered compromise of 1975, which ended mutual subversion and provided a border settlement between Iraq and Iran. The second is the Algerian-mediated settlement of the US hostage crisis, which concluded in January 1981. Today, however, the Algerians are too identified with Iran to be acceptable as mediators with Iraq. The earlier Algiers accord between the Shah's regime and Iraq did not face some of the current ideological aspects of the dispute and was violated by both sides at the first opportunity. The hostage-crisis negotiations do indicate, though, that Iran can show flexibility when faced with continuation of an unprofitable conflict. Both negotiations also may demonstrate that a single mediator, perceived as balanced and trusted by both sides, may be more effective than multistate agencies in dealing with these two countries.

The UN as a Potential Mediator

International organizations are often acceptable as mediators of conflicts because they are perceived as neutral and disinterested by those involved in the dispute. Both Iran and Iraq ask, as would their counterparts in other problems, what the bias is of any given actor. In this case, Iran views the international order as illegitimate and as intrinsically biased against it. In Tehran's eyes, therefore, the United Nations may be representative of the world order—or consensus—but that is a disadvantage, not an asset. Iran also views the international structure and the United Nations itself as US-dominated.

This brings us to a second problem facing the United Nations as a potential mediator. An international organization's other asset may be its track record—its proven ability to be fair and to settle disputes. From the Iranian point of view, though, the UN record is not seen as promising. The organization clearly, and properly, opposed Tehran's stand on the hostage crisis, and the Security Council called three times for the release of the US diplomats. UN Secretary General Kurt Waldheim's visit to Tehran over the hostage issue was also met with Iranian antagonism. Further, Iranian leaders feel the UN's failure to condemn Iraq as the aggressor in 1980 was a hostile act.

While the United Nations might be extremely helpful in secondary issues—cleaning up a serious oil spill, barring attacks on civilian targets, observing and investigating the situation—it is unlikely to play a central role on the main question of resolving the war. Such more-limited successes, though, may somewhat soften Iranian mistrust, and a channel has been opened that might help in the case of broader negotiations.

The most promising multilateral effort has been the work of the Islamic Conference Organization's Peace Committee. As an Islamic organization, the forty-five-member ICO is acceptable to Iran. Its leaders, particularly Habib Chatti, have traveled frequently to both capitals offering their services and drawing hope from occasional hints of flexibility from Tehran. Yet on exploration, each feeler proved fruitless, and Iran has even condemned the ICO. As one Tehran leader put it in July 1984 in remarks that also apply to Iranian attitudes to the United Nations, "If the committee thinks it is making an effort for peace with all the faults which exist in some of its members and the stands they have taken in favor of the aggressor, it is making a big mistake. One side has launched an aggression and the other has faced an aggression. One side has used chemical bombs and the other has suffered human losses from these bombings. One side has destroyed cities with long-range missiles and the other has had thousands of martyrs."

Possibilities for Managing the Conflict

If the United Nations has meager prospects as a mediator, it has had some limited success in "managing" the conflict. Prospects for such management in the future, however limited, seem brighter than prospects for resolution of the conflict. Although Iran has not favored a negotiated end to the war, both Tehran and Baghdad have, throughout the changing fortunes of battle, favored limitations on it. Obviously, the outside world has also had a considerable interest in preventing the war from sparking an even wider conflict.

Swedish Prime Minister Palme, as representative of the UN Secretary General, undertook efforts to work out limits to the conflict during the 1980–1982 period. His proposals called for a cease-fire, Iraqi withdrawal from Iranian territory, and negotiations. He was not successful, and it was evident that the time was not ripe for progress in this direction. A pause in such concerted efforts followed.

Even during that early period there were also initiatives on narrower points. In 1981, for example, UN representatives almost succeeded in working out arrangements for the departure of ships trapped by the war in the Shatt al-Arab waterway. In furtherance of its claim to the entire waterway, however, Iraq wanted to pay the entire costs, while Iran, claiming half of the Shatt, insisted on paying half of the costs. The arrangement broke down.

By 1984, though, damage-control attempts bore fruit on several points. The United Nations succeeded in organizing a moratorium of attacks on civilian population centers after both sides accepted an appeal from the Secretary General in June 1984. Its on-the-spot investigation of the culpability of such attacks was used by both sides for propaganda, but it also embarrassed them by pointing to their abuses. The stationing of UN teams to check on attacks also helped limit such attacks in the second half of 1984. The moratorium broke down in early 1985, however, and attacks against cities by both sides escalated in the spring of 1985.

Attempts to prevent the use of chemical weapons may also have been effective temporarily, though on a de facto basis. Following an Iranian offensive of October 1983, there were reports that Iraq had used such weapons in violation of the Geneva Protocol of 1925, to which it was a signatory. Iran requested the UN Secretary General to send a mission to investigate. Iraq refused to approve the mission, however, and UN Secretary General Javier Pérez de Cuéllar, in accordance with his practice respecting this conflict, declined Iran's request on the grounds that it had not been accepted by both combatants. Iran thereupon held a medical conference of its own in Tehran, at which European doctors concluded that Iraq had used mustard gas.

Fighting in February 1984 led to new reports of the Iraqi use of chemical weapons. This time the Secretary General acted without Iraqi agreement and dispatched a team of experts to Iran in March. The mission concluded that mustard gas and nerve gas had been used. On the strength of its report, the Secretary General deplored the use of chemical weapons, and the president of the Security Council issued a statement on behalf of its members strongly condemning the violations of the Geneva Protocol. The United States and Britain banned the sale to Iraq of several compounds used to make chemical weapons, although they continued to be available on the international market. Iraq denied again that it had used such weapons. Despite its unwillingness to acknowledge use or to agree to a ban on use, Iraq refrained from employing chemical weapons until the general escalation of warfare in the spring of 1985, when evidence accumulated of renewed use by Baghdad.

Another element in limiting the consequences of the conflict was the protection of prisoners-of-war. This issue has been handled mostly by the International Committee of the Red Cross, and the United Nations was inclined to leave the issue in its hands despite requests by Iraq to send a mission. However, in October 1984, after International Red Cross officials witnessed a riot in one of Iran's prisoner camps in which several Iraqis died, the United Nations obtained the agreement of Tehran and Baghdad for a mission to visit both countries to observe treatment of prisoners. The UN team carried out its visits in January 1985, reporting some abuses in both countries. In its report it recommended the release of as many prisoners as possible on both sides. Neither side agreed, but both did release limited numbers of disabled prisoners.

Even in this passionate and bloody war, fear of reprisal or of international pressure is still a potent force in preserving limits. Both Iran and Iraq are capable of inflicting much more damage on each other than they have hitherto done. Each of the combatant's determination to use international mediation efforts for propaganda has sometimes led to frustrating failures over imagery. At the same time, however, this competition has also led to some degree of cooperation to gain public favor abroad and to portray the other side as recalcitrant. This situation has provided mediators with some leverage of their own.

Implicitly, at least, the United Nations and other third-party negotiators have also suggested ways in which limits on the conflict could furnish a transitional program for ending it in practice through the creation of a "de facto peace." Such efforts have had the following components: helping other states remain neutral and unaffected by the conflict to the greatest possible extent; preserving free navigation; protecting the rights of civilians and prisoners-of-war; and avoiding escalation to new types of weapons that would cause high nonmilitary casualties. The most developed of these efforts—the United Nations calls it an "incremental approach"—was a Japanese-handled initiative that ended without success in September 1984. This initiative hoped to build on the civilian protection and anti-chemical-warfare appeals. A proposed agreement to cease attacks on vessels in the Gulf, aimed at stopping Iraqi planes from sinking Iran-bound tankers, was to be combined with an Iranian willingness to allow tankers to use Iraqi ports, which have been closed since the beginning of the war. Even if Iran wanted to avoid actually making peace, such measures could in the future offer face-saving ways out of the current impasse.

Given the deadlock on the battlefield, it is conceivable that even without any mediatory efforts the war may in time become a "phony war" situation such as existed in Europe in early 1940. Iranian and Iraqi soldiers would still confront each other in the trenches; but without attacks on civilian cities behind the lines, major offensives, or the naval aspect of the conflict, the war would be more symbolic than real.

Other areas that could be investigated to circumscribe the war include: international cooperation against airplane hijackings, clarifying the terms of the naval engagement, and mutual limits on attacking petroleum installations.

Lessons for the Future

In some ways, the Iran-Iraq war is a very traditional conflict between two states over spheres of influence, border territory, and mutual hostility concerning specific issues. At the same time, it has an important ethnic and ideological component leading to each side's broad-ranging goal of deposing the other's political system. The latter characteristic makes it a difficult conflict to mediate. The two belligerents also have interests, however, which would be served by restricting the conflict in certain ways.

Third parties must analyze the conflict on two levels, considering the possibility for a negotiated settlement while seeking management of the conflict. Channels might be found to move from the latter to the former.

Another general lesson is the need for courageous persistence on the part of international organizations and agencies. For example, by its actual performance in the field, the UN Secretariat has succeeded in reducing Iran's mistrust, which was engendered by actions of the UN's membership bodies. Just because an approach fails the first time—or the first dozen times—it is tried does not mean that progress cannot be made in future efforts.

The following points might also be kept in mind:

- Both Iran and Iraq have had opportunities to try for all-out victory on the battlefield, and these efforts have failed. Their subjective consciousness must catch up to this objective reality.
- Since triumph has not materalized, mediators may seek face-saving measures that allow each side to claim victory while helping Iran and Iraq find their way to peace.
- Peace can be de facto as well as de jure, and a deadlock on the battlefield is conducive to efforts to limit the war.
- Efforts to prevent expansion of the war have in their favor the fact that both sides see expansion as against their interest. Third-party management can assure each side of restraints on the opponent and can provide the parties with excuses for putting a ceiling on the types of weapons and the locations of attacks. This tends to prevent preemptive escalations.
- Even those most contemptuous of international public opinion or the norms of state behavior can be led to shape their behavior by leverage based on such considerations.

Bibliography

Cordesman, Anthony. *The Gulf and the Search for Strategic Stability.* Boulder, Colorado: Westview Press, 1984.

Cottrell, Alvin, ed. *The Persian Gulf States: A General Survey.* Baltimore: Johns Hopkins University Press, 1980.

Heller, Mark. "The Iran-Iraq War: Implications for Third Parties." Jaffee Center for Strategic Studies, Tel Aviv University, Paper No. 23, January 1984.

Hussein, Amirsadeghi, ed. *Security Dimensions in the Persian Gulf.* London: St. Martin's Press, Inc., 1981.

Rubin, Barry. *Paved with Good Intentions: The American Experience and Iran.* New York: Oxford University Press, 1980.

Security in the Persian Gulf, Vols. I–IV. London: Institute of Strategic Studies, 1982.

Tahrir-Kheli, Shirin. *The Iran-Iraq War: Old Conflicts, New Weapons.* New York: Praeger Publishers, 1983.

Zabih, Sepher. *Iran Since the Revolution.* Baltimore: Johns Hopkins University Press, 1982.

IV

Multilateral Approaches to Multidimensional Conflict Resolution: Lessons from the Horn of Africa

John W. Harbeson

Introduction

If there is one defining feature of the long-standing conflict between Ethiopia and Somalia, it is multidimensionality. First, the struggle involves local, regional, and global powers. Second, the border dispute between Ethiopia and Somalia that is the immediate problem has been closely intertwined with a number of other issues in the Horn of Africa. Third, this related set of issues bridges, even breaks down the distinction between, the "international" and "domestic" arenas. Finally, the immediate political-military conflict over the Ethiopian-Somali border is enmeshed in broader problems of socioeconomic rehabilitation and development involving not only refugees but the well-being of some of the globe's poorest countries.

Periodic open warfare between Ethiopia and Somalia over the border presents the impression of specifically regional international conflict at a particular time between established actors whose interests are defined, consequential, and irreconcilable. In fact the conflict is nothing of the kind, and "multidimensionality" sums up the complexities and ambiguities that lie barely beneath the surface in the Horn of Africa. In these circumstances, it is possible that regional organizations such as, in this case, the Organization of African Unity (OAU) may best be able to address the complex, interrelated regional issues more effectively than global organizations such as the United Nations. Somewhat paradoxically, the validity of such a proposition may depend on tacit superpower

John W. Harbeson is director of international studies at City College of New York and professor of political science at the Graduate Center of the City University of New York. He has written extensively on revolution and development in the Horn of Africa and on rural development in eastern and southern Africa.

concurrence that their direct competition in the given area is of secondary rather than primary importance.

Tension and strife between Ethiopia and Somalia are at first blush regional in scope and focus, but all the nations of the continent at a minimum have an interest in how the issues involved are resolved or are not resolved. The geographical boundaries of the Horn of Africa are more clearly defined and more commonly accepted than the political ones, which do not sharply distinguish this theater from those of the Indian Ocean, the Middle East, and North Africa. Moreover, the boundary between "international" and "domestic" politics in the Horn of Africa is imprecise at best, perhaps nearly nonexistent. One important reason is that the very definition of "Ethiopia" has been the focus of armed conflict for at least a quarter of a century, especially since the removal from power of Emperor Haile Selassie I. The difference between "cold" and "hot" war in the relationships between Ethiopia and Somalia has been blurred, as has the origin of the struggle itself, in the machinations of European imperial powers and an African empire to define the region and the actors that were to play upon this stage. Finally, the theater of diplomatic and military struggle cannot be treated in isolation from the effects of extreme poverty, one clear common denominator in the region, or from the struggles of all parties to promote development and to raise standards of living. Resolution of the broader dispute competes with desperate struggles for development in both countries.

A primary result of the multiple ambiguities characterizing the Horn of Africa is that the definition of the interests at stake, as well as their importance and reconcilability, is imprecise and uncertain. On one level the basic issue is clear enough: where to draw the border to the pastoralists who inhabit the area is uncertain. The wishes of those whose citizenship would be affected by a redrawing of the border are unclear in part because their loyalties to the "national" regimes in either Mogadiscio or Addis Ababa are at best qualified. In short, the actors involved, the interests at stake, and the theater of conflict itself are profoundly ill-defined, so that those who would promote peace in the area must deal simultaneously with many overlapping dimensions of conflict.

This paper presents two principal hypotheses. First, the very multidimensionality of the conflict has served to diminish the possibilities of escalation, while the responses of the principal regional actors to the multidimensionality of the conflict have led to a reduced likelihood of superpower confrontation in the Horn of Africa. Such responses appear to have been accepted and/or encouraged by the superpowers.

Second, the multidimensionality of the Ethiopia-Somalia conflict presents both barriers and possibly unexplored opportunities for multilateral conflict management. To the degree that conflict-management efforts presume definition of actors and interest and delineation of the zone within which they are in conflict, the Ethiopia-Somalia conflict may only now be evolving into a stage where formal conflict management is possible, the seriousness and intensity of the problems involved notwithstanding. Initiatives by the local regional actors themselves, acting in their own self-interest as they perceive it, may be a prerequisite for successful management in such circumstances.

Alternatively, the situation in the Horn of Africa may be fairly representative of international conflict among the world's poorer and generally newer nations and, thus, a challenge to evolve new forms of mediation more appropriate to such circumstances. Moreover, the very multidimensional ambiguity of international conflict in the Horn may indicate resources for, as well as obstacles to, negotiation. In spite of the intensity of the struggle, such ambiguities may signify degrees of diplomatic freedom and flexibility that appropriately fashioned diplomatic efforts might utilize in resolving international differences. One basic issue, therefore, is how well placed multilateral agencies are to evolve forms of mediation suited to utilizing the particular resources as well as to addressing the particular issues characteristic of international relations in developing nations. This article suggests that where the issues and indeed the definition of the actors themselves have not crystallized and become clearly distinct from one another, regional actors such as the Organization of African Unity may be in a better position, at a minimum, to be a forum in which the issues can be discussed informally.

This paper explores these hypotheses separately in its first two sections. In the concluding section, some possible lessons and insights for multilateral conflict management of multidimensional conflicts in developing countries are suggested, drawing on the Horn of Africa experience.

Multidimensionality in the Horn: Circumstances and Response

Circumstances of Multidimensionality

Ethiopia and Somalia do not agree on the border between their two countries. Ethiopia and Kenya both claim jurisdiction over peoples who are ethnic Somalis. As is true for nearly all of the African continent, "national" borders were established largely through negotiation and competition among the European powers during the period of their imperial expansion. The Horn of Africa is distinctive in that Ethiopian emperors were also engaged in territorial expansion and were party to the negotiations resulting in political borders in northeastern Africa as the borders now appear on most maps. Somalia would redraw those maps to include within its borders Somali communities currently resident within Ethiopia and Kenya. The last full-scale warfare over the issue occurred in late 1977 between Ethiopia and Somalia, punctuating periods of armed tension and border skirmishes that have continued ever since and that had gone on for many years before over this unresolved issue.

Periods of the greatest tension and conflict between Somalia and its neighbors have appeared to follow in the wake of the greatest internal transformations within Ethiopia and Kenya: the Anglo-Ethiopian treaty confirming Ethiopian control over the Somali-populated Ogaden region in 1897 during a period of large-scale Ethiopian territorial expansion; the restoration of Haile Selassie to the Ethiopian throne, ending Italy's World War II occupation of the country; Kenya's independence at the end of 1963; and the beginnings of the Ethiopian revolution in 1974. However, perhaps because inclusion of Somali-inhabited districts within Kenya was the work of Britain and not of an independent Kenyan government, the Kenya-Somalia struggle has generally been less intense than that between Ethiopia and Somalia. Nevertheless, Kenya has for many years cooperated with Ethiopia in restraining what both countries consider to be Somali irredentism. The potential for oil and gas discovery in both the Ogaden and the Kenya northeastern province has added an additional dimension to the conflict, one that has proved secondary due to the meager results of oil-company prospecting to date.

The Actors: Capabilities, Interests, Responses

There are several categories of actors in the Ethiopia-Somalia conflict: primary states, peripheral states, sub-national groupings, extra-regional powers, superpowers, and multilateral agencies.

Primary State Actors. First, there are the primary state actors, Ethiopia and Somalia. The two countries are vastly disproportionate in size and area. Ethiopia covers an area nearly twice the size of Somalia, and has a population estimated at around forty million, compared to Somalia's approximately five million. It will be shown, however, that uncertain definition of the actors and the interrelatedness of the international issues in the Horn serve to diminish the prima facie significance of these differences.

The presumption is that the conflict has persisted between two established nation-states, each with the authority to continue or to negotiate the conflict on behalf of those domiciled within its respective borders. The two states are both among the poorest in the developing world, with gross national products per capita estimated at $140 for Ethiopia and $280 for Somalia. At the same time, they have maintained some of the largest armed forces on the continent. Ethiopia's 250,000-person Army trails only Egypt, and in 1983, the Mengistu regime introduced compulsory military service. Somalia's armed forces are but a fraction as large, at 54,000, but it still ranks eighth after Egypt, Ethiopia, Nigeria, Morocco, Algeria, the Republic of South Africa, and the Sudan. The underlying poverty of the two countries is reflected in the relative size of their domestic defense expenditures, which places Ethiopia only seventh and Somalia seventeenth among the countries of the continent. Ethiopia and Somalia are both among the most militarized states in Africa. Somalia led the list in 1978 with nearly 16 percent of the population in its armed forces, while Ethiopia ranked third behind Guinea-Bissau at 7.5 percent, a rate which will dramatically increase as universal military service takes effect. Both are among the most active participants in international arms transfers. Between 1978 and 1982, Ethiopia received over $2.4 billion in arms, virtually all of it from the Soviet Union, and was the third biggest arms recipient after Libya and Algeria. Somalia ranked eighth during this period, at $675 million.

Calculation of a balance of power between Ethiopia and Somalia is at best difficult but would appear to favor Ethiopia were it not for the civil strife and the secessionist-movement pressures that have wracked Ethiopia since the beginning of the revolution in 1974. Ethiopia houses eight times the population of Somalia. Though poorer in per capita income, Ethiopia appears to have substantially greater economic potential. Its armed forces, as we have seen, are much larger and are supported far more generously by arms transfers and military technical assistance. Ethiopia's Air Force appears to be larger and better equipped than Somalia's, particularly since the massive infusion of Soviet military assistance. Armed forces morale is a potential problem in both countries. Somali officers have been reported disappointed that US military assistance has been much below that previously provided by the Soviet government. There have been periodic reports of grumbling within the Ethiopian military over levels of compensation and over the difficulty and unpleasantness of fighting "domestic" insurgent groups. Problems of this nature helped spark the 1974 military takeover in the first place.

Any military advantage that Ethiopia may enjoy on paper has been neutralized during much of the past decade by internal struggles that appear to have been far more costly and debilitating with respect to military capability than has been the case for Somalia. The Ethiopian armed forces, even with massive Soviet and, until recently, Cuban assistance, have been able to maintain only a stalemate against sometimes unified, sometimes mutually antagonistic Eritrean liberation movements. The Addis Ababa government's writ has run only intermittently in northern regions south of Eritrea. In many of the southern provinces, other than in the Ogaden itself, liberation movements have flourished, linked to some uncertain and unequal degree under the banner of the Oromo Liberation Front (OLF). In the capital city itself, groups opposed to the government of Mengistu Haile Mariam are quiescent rather than extinguished. Even within the armed forces there have been periodic rumblings of discontent with Mengistu's leadership of the country. The situation is that the government appears to have contained but not to have eliminated such opposition, the presence of which is at the very least a major distraction for the Mengistu government in its effort to deal effectively wth Somalia.

Central to understanding the multidimensionality of the Ethiopia-Somalia conflict is the recognition that those groups in opposition within Ethiopia, including but not limited to those operating in the Ogaden, appear to seek more than a change of government or policy. Many of these groups do not object to and even welcome such measures as rural land reform and literacy training, but nevertheless appear unreconciled to the continued existence of Ethiopia per se. Their agenda is to roll back the empire reestablished and enlarged by Emperor Menelik II and his predecessors in the late nineteenth and twentieth centuries. Were negotiation to be established between such groups and the Mengistu government, they might or might not accept something short of full independence. The result is that while Somalia's dispute is with Ethiopia, it is not clear who within Ethiopia recognizes "Ethiopia" for the purposes of this dispute or for any other reason.

Ethiopia's condition, therefore, changes drastically the dimensions of what is intrinsically a local issue. Blurring of the distinction between "international" and "domestic" disputes results not only from the presence of ethnic Somalis within Ethiopia but also from the fact that any potential concession to them by the Addis Ababa government directly affects the legitimacy of the state itself as well as the government. The local border issue is, therefore, not easily separable from much larger issues, ones with which the interests of other regional and non-regional powers are inescapably involved.

Thus enlarged, the local border dispute becomes simultaneously a "domestic" and an "international" issue. Domestically it involves ethnicity, region, and class, for the peoples of the Ogaden are ethnically distinct, politically peripheral within Ethiopia, and economically poor even by Ethiopian standards. Their "colonization" by Menelik established a structure of class stratification that the removal of the emperor per se did not appear to these peoples to eliminate. The important reforms introduced by the military government have not removed these issues in the eyes of many communities because they have not been accompanied by the acceptance of increased autonomy nor have they in practice,

rhetoric notwithstanding, taken into account the special requirements
of local economies such as those of the pastoralists who are prevalent
in the Ogaden region.

The local border conflict becomes an international issue in several
ways. It is an anti-colonial conflict in that: (1) the existing provisional
boundaries were established by European colonial powers, were reestablished after World War II, and were confirmed prior to Somalia's
independence; and (2) an African empire led by Menelik II enlarged
its sphere at the expense of Somalia and, from a Somali perspective,
did so in cooperation with European empires. Somalia's pursuit of its
border claims challenges the nearly continent-wide consensus, reflected
consistently by the Organization of African Unity, that any rearrangement
of colonially defined orders sets an unacceptable precedent in a region
of arbitrarily defined national borders and regimes of already precarious
stability. Finally, linkage between Somali irredentism and the potential
balkanization of the dominant military power in the region increases
the bearing of the issue on the adjacent Middle East and Indian Ocean
theaters and on the regional as well as the superpower interests involved
in them.

The multidimensionality of the conflict circumscribes the options
immediately available to both countries. Any Ethiopian-government
concession of increased formal autonomy to Somalis in the Ogaden as
a result of Somali military pressure would lend strength to the insurgent
groups, which the Mengistu regime can contain only with difficulty
even now. The Mengistu government's response on all fronts, therefore,
has been to preserve the empire by force where necessary in order to
transform it. In an odd parody of Rousseau's teachings in *The Social
Contract*, the military regime has sought to force all communities to
adhere to the empire in order to be liberated within it by the major
reforms the government has initiated. With or without the help of other
powers, Ethiopia must find a way to detach the struggle over its "external"
borders from the struggle over the "internal" redefinition of the empire
in order to acquire flexibility to address the Somali issue. As we shall
see below, the changing posture of the Western Somali Liberation Front
(WSLF) suggests that such differentiation of the internal and external
struggles may be under way.

Somalia also lacks options. The fundamental reason is that while the
ethnic unity of Somalia within its present borders exceeds that of
virtually all African states, those borders have been not only arbitrarily
defined but unstable. In the 1880's, Britain's argument with France over
the assignment of Djibouti to France's administration (a partitioning of
Somalia, from the Somali nationalist perspective) reflected British uncertainty over the true boundaries of "Somalia." Britain withdrew its

claims to lands west of the present border without actually ceding them to Ethiopia; Britain, Italy, and Ethiopia failed to reconcile their understandings concerning the boundary; and none of the parties made much effort to establish the border in the minds of the pastoralists of the region.[1] In the years prior to the Italian occupation in 1936, Italy encouraged Somali incursions into Ethiopia because such were consistent with Il Duce's own designs. Italian control of both countries in the early part of World War II, subsequent British occupation, and the postwar combination of Ethiopian pressure on borders and Allied-power debates over how to administer the area diminished the political significance of the boundaries. The citizenship of Somalis in northeastern Kenya was not resolved without debate even by Britain itself as it prepared to grant Kenya independence.

In short, one important reason why Somali nationalism has not been defined to be coterminous with the existing boundaries was the failure of several empires to agree among themselves during the period of their hegemony on what those borders should be. Somali nationalists, therefore, were never effectively deterred from defining the political boundaries of Somalia to be coincident with the de facto ethnic ones. The result has been that President Mohamed Siad Barre and his predecessors have risked appearing less nationalistic to their own people to the extent that they have accepted restricted national boundaries. This has especially been the case since the homeland of Siad Barre and, particularly recently, of many of his advisers, lies in the Ogaden beyond the country's de facto borders. The existence of the Somali state does not hinge on the resolution of the border dispute, as it may for Ethiopia, but the legitimacy of any Somali administration is affected. The apparent shakiness of Siad Barre's regime at times since the 1977 war is a result of many factors in addition to losing the war. One fundamental reason, however, appears to be that historically ill-defined boundaries meant that the limitation of Somali jurisdiction and sovereignty could not easily be separated from the loss of national identity.

In a cruelly ironic way, the massive Soviet-supported Ethiopian counterattack against invading Somali forces in the 1977 war may have increased rather than decreased the Somali government's freedom of action in its dealings with Ethiopia over the Ogaden. After the bitterness of defeat in the 1977 war began to ease, the lasting effect of the war may have been that the boundary was more decisively established than at any time in the preceding hundred years. Has Somali nationalism finally been given a context, however arbitrary and costly, that other African states have "enjoyed" for most of the twentieth century? Sharper, more decisive definition of Somali boundaries may possibly allow the Somali government the flexibility to support Somali self-determination in Ethiopia without necessarily insisting on claiming these Somali peoples for the Somali nation-state.

Peripheral State Actors. Second, there are peripheral state actors. These are neighboring states that are not directly party to the controversy but whose interests are nevertheless directly affected by the outcome and that may, therefore, be allied with one of the primary state actors rather than neutral. These states include Kenya, the Sudan, and Djibouti.

Kenya has fought with insurgent Somalis over the disposition of its northeastern district, but in recent years the ongoing tension in this area has paled by comparison to that between the primary nation-state actors. Kenya has been relatively successful among African states in the quest for development, having risen to middle-income status by some analyses. Kenya's per capita income was estimated at $420 in 1981, half again that of Somalia and three times that of Ethiopia. The 1982 coup attempt notwithstanding, Kenya has remained one of the more stable of African states and one, moreover, that has retained more political freedom and a more significant role for its legislature than has been true for most countries of the continent. Kenya is beset by continuing problems that have the potential for spilling over into the region but appear unlikely to do so in the immediately foreseeable future: difficulties over land use and allocation, very heavy population pressure on limited good-quality land, sustaining the multi-ethnic coalition under President Daniel arap Moi forged by founding President Jomo Kenyatta, political corruption, and an underlying problem of political identity intensified by the dominant role of Western foreign investment and its accompanying culture.

Military expenditure in Kenya has been among the most rapidly growing in the region. Military expenditure as a percentage of gross national product tripled between 1972 and 1980 from a low of 1.3 percent to an average of 4.4 percent. Between 1978 and 1982, the value of arms transfers to Kenya totaled approximately $400 million, the high average for the continent. Significantly, its arms imports were relatively diversified, the largest percentage originating from the United States but with important imports also from France, Britain, and Italy. While the size of its armed forces doubled during the 1970's, its 13,000-person contingent is but a fraction of Ethiopia's and Somalia's.

The fairly rapid expansion of Kenya's military establishment is related to the country's isolation within the region. Until late 1983, a closed border with Tanzania bespoke ongoing ideological tensions between the two countries that were exacerbated by Kenya's relative economic strength and by the fact that each harbored the other's political dissidents. Since the appearance of Idi Amin in Uganda and also since his downfall, instability in Uganda has been a further source of concern to Kenya, which was aggravated by Tanzania's military involvement in ending the Amin regime. Only with its northern neighbors, Ethiopia and the Sudan, has Kenya enjoyed relatively untroubled relations, in spite of southern-based opposition movements in both countries.

Especially under President arap Moi, Kenya has sought to further domestic political stability. To the extent it can be achieved, such stability might allow the country to diminish its vulnerability to sources of regional instability. Arap Moi's extended chairmanship of the OAU may have facilitated this implicit strategy. After prolonged negotiations, Kenya and Tanzania reopened their borders in the fall of 1983 following six years of closure, and the first tentative steps were taken by Uganda, Tanzania, and Kenya to negotiate assignment of the assets of the defunct East African Economic Community.

Similarly, Kenya has moved to diminish the tension between its regional alignments and its global affiliations. It has maintained close cooperation with Ethiopia despite heavy Soviet military investment in the Mengistu regime and has wrestled with Somalia over the fate of the northeastern district, while the United States has been the major military patron of both Kenya and Somalia. Although it has mobilized Somalis in the northeastern province to renounce union with Somalia publicly and benefited from the loyalty of Somali officers during the 1982 coup attempt, Kenya has at the same time moved to establish more normal relations with Somalia. These attempts have been reflected in Somali cooperation on cross-border cattle raids and the Mogadiscio government's specific denial that it seeks to detach the northeastern province from Kenya. While the United States may well have encouraged and facilitated a Kenya-Somalia rapprochement, the initiative appears to be consistent with Kenya's perception of its own regional interest.

At the same time, Kenya has done nothing to reduce cooperation with the Mengistu government in Ethiopia, one tangible measure of which has been the completion of a road linking Addis Ababa and Nairobi. Kenya's ties with Ethiopia have been maintained despite Ethiopia's accusation that the United States has sought to encircle the country through stepped-up military assistance to the Sudan and Somalia as well as to Kenya. While staunchly pro-Western in domestic policy and international alignment, Kenya has taken care that its Western military assistance emanates from several sources. Although it has been one of the largest recipients of US military assistance, Kenya has maintained correct if somewhat formal relations with the Soviet Union. Kenya's support for a United Nations–sponsored "zone of peace" in the Indian Ocean has helped reinforce Kenya's posture as a nonaligned nation.

Kenya's interests appear, thus, to lie in reducing the multidimensionality of the Ethiopia-Somalia dispute. By moving toward a regional middle ground, Kenya in effect seeks to define the boundaries of the dispute more clearly, i.e., to include Ethiopia and Somalia but not itself. By moving to soften the tension between its regional alignments and global orientations, Kenya implicitly seeks to distance itself at least marginally from superpower competition in the Horn. Kenya's quest for a balanced regional posture is in the country's domestic interests as well, for it reduces the likelihood that the politics of the Horn will deepen serious and long-term domestic political cleavages. Putting some distance between itself and the politics of the Horn may also enable Kenya to prevent regional struggles from diverting resources from its already difficult struggle to maintain a relatively strong pattern of economic growth.

The character of internal politics in tiny Djibouti cannot but be strongly influenced by the primary states' relationship, given its delicate internal ethnic balance between predominantly Ethiopian-oriented Afars and generally Somali-oriented Issas. The government of President Hassan Gouled Aptidon has also sought to enhance fragile domestic political stability by moving toward nonalignment in as many dimensions of the Ethiopia-Somalia struggle as possible. The country's economic development depends critically on the rail line to Addis Ababa, over which trade through its airport and harbor flows to and from the interior. Having failed to maintain an internal multi-ethnic political coalition of Afars as well as Issas, the Djibouti government has established friendship and cooperation treaties externally with the countries in the region that tend to be at least sympathetic with the internal claims of the Afars (Ethiopia) and the Issas (Somalia). In this way the government has sought to moderate the impact of Ethiopian-Somali tensions on those between Afars and Issas domestically. The treaty with Somalia, in particular, represents substantial renunciation of Somalia's claims to Djibouti on ethnic grounds. The treaty with Ethiopia includes agreement to maintain the Djibouti–Addis Ababa railway link vital to both countries and a promise from Addis Ababa not to interfere in Djibouti's internal politics so long as Djibouti does not allow dissident Afars from Ethiopia to take refuge and to make common cause with those in Djibouti.

The Sudan is the only peripheral state not directly affected by the Ethiopia-Somalia border dispute. It is nevertheless more than indirectly involved because of its troubled relationship with one of the primary state actors, Ethiopia, and because of its linkage with Somalia and Kenya through common participation in security agreements with the United States, which Soviet-backed Ethiopia views as a policy of encirclement. The Sudan and Ethiopia share a border only somewhat less ambiguously defined than that between Ethiopia and Somalia. Ethiopia and the Sudan have accused one another of promoting strong separatist movements that have seriously weakened the stability and legitimacy of the respective regimes. The Sudan has harbored Eritrean refugees as well as those from other northern and western Ethiopian provinces. Ethiopia has appeared to support one of the southern-based Sudanese opposition groups, The Sudanese People's Liberation Army, which sought alliances with northern dissidents in order to overthrow the regime of President Gaafar Muhammed Nimeiri rather than cooperating with a rival southern insurgency that was promoting secession. Its posture since the overthrow of Nimeiri had not become clear when this article was written.

The Sudan has acted recently to define the boundaries of the Ethiopia-Somalia dispute more distinctly through increased isolation from all parties rather than through regional nonalignment. The Nimeiri government's precipitate declaration in the fall of 1983 that the Sudan would become a full-fledged Islamic state may intensify the domestic cleavage between the Moslem north and the predominantly non-Moslem south, while confusing the Sudan's regional relations. The declaration appears simultaneously to neutralize pro-Libyan elements; to antagonize Ethiopia, which has sought to diffuse the religious issue; and to confuse Ethiopian dissidents, to whom it may offer support but who adhere either to some form of Christianity or to less fundamentalist versions of Islam. The declaration may well strain whatever commonality of strategic interests that exists between the Sudan and Kenya, Somalia, and Egypt, none of which wishes to encourage radical Islamic movements. The new post-Nimeiri government did not give any early indication of modifying this strategy.

Sub-national Actors. Third, there are sub-national actors whose behavior and defined interests are at least partially independent of and distinct from those of the primary or peripheral state actors. The number and loyalty of their constituents, the geographical boundaries within which their writ runs, and the character of their relationship to the primary and peripheral state actors are not sharply defined. One such set of actors includes the Democratic Front for the Salvation of Somalia and the Somali National Movement, which from apparently distinct regional bases within Somalia are backed by Ethiopia in their quest to overthrow the regime of Siad Barre. Both are vague about the specific disposition of the Ogaden. Both also, through their opposition to the Camp David accords, have signaled their intent to realign Somalia within the adjacent Middle East theater.

A second species of sub-national actors, with more ambiguous and changing aims and relationships to a primary actor, is represented by the Western Somali Liberation Front. The WSLF was actively supported by Somali regular troops in the 1977 Ethiopian-Somali war toward the end of detaching the Ogaden from Ethiopia. Since then the organization has become estranged from Somalia, while seeking a more vaguely defined regional self-determination, although at the cost of an important split within its ranks. One reason for the change is the existence of a third form of sub-national actor represented by the Oromo Liberation Front. During the high tide of Somali incursion into Ethiopia, the Mogadiscio government sought to make common cause with the communities linked under the Oromo banner in a joint effort to end colonial subservience to Addis Ababa, a subservience perpetuated in their view by the military successors to Haile Selassie. But the OLF viewed WSLF linkage to the Somali government as contrary to, and perhaps a threat to, its quest for self-determination from Addis Ababa, reinforcing what may be underemphasized ethnic differentiation between and within the groups.

The changing position of the WSLF is of critical importance to the definition of the Ethiopia-Somalia context. To the extent that the WSLF continues to evolve toward a more vaguely defined pursuit of self-determination vis-à-vis Addis Ababa and away from demonstrable Somali support, the multidimensional Ethiopia-Somalia struggle becomes more one-dimensional: clarification of a boundary rather than a zero-sum contest between an African nationalist movement and an African empire. At the same time, WSLF movement toward the posture of the OLF sharpens the question of the linkage between northern and southern sub-national actors, each of which seeks the redefinition of Ethiopia. At present, common cause between the Eritrean and Tigre liberation movements and those of the WSLF and the OLF appears to be foundering, somewhat ironically, because of the legacy of the empire each seeks to dismantle. The OLF views the northern groups with some suspicion because it believes they have not disavowed the policies of the regime, against which they struggle, that prompted and perpetuated colonization of the south. The result is that the legacy of empire has thus far prevented the two groups of partisans from linking their external supporters of "self-determination," the Sudan and Somalia, in a united effort to redefine Ethiopia.

Extra-regional Powers. A fourth category of actors is made up of extra-regional powers. These are nation-state actors geographically outside the main theater of conflict bounding the first three groups of actors. They are primarily in the Arab world. The involvement of Arab states with primary, peripheral, and sub-national actors links the Ethiopia-Somalia dispute to the broader issues raging in the Middle East and therefore to the interests of the superpowers. The effect of such engagement has been to reinforce existing divisions within the Arab world. Libya and South Yemen have established a tripartite alliance with Ethiopia. From Ethiopia's perspective, such an alliance permits it to encircle its encirclers. This tripartite agreement put particular pressure on the Sudan, which, along with Egypt, underwent a period of ostracism within the Arab world following the Camp David accords. It is still not clear, however, the extent to which this tripartite alignment has produced tangible, material support for the Mengistu government as distinct from symbolic support for propaganda purposes.

From the standpoint of South Yemen, the tripartite alliance may help to overcome its own isolation as a radical state within a region of more conservative states on the Arabian peninsula. Libya, on the other hand, welcomed cooperation with Ethiopia as a means of putting increased pressure on the Nimeiri regime, which Libyan leader Colonel Muammar el-Qaddafi would like to see overthrown not least because of its Western orientation and support for the Camp David accords. Again, at this writing, Libyan posture had not yet become clear toward the successor regime in the Sudan. At the same time, competition among Eritrean groups for supremacy has further divided more conservative and more radical Arab states. Saudi Arabia, meantime, was one of the principal architects of Somalia's separation from its Soviet patron just as the war with Ethiopia was intensifying and has continued financial and military support for Somalia's postwar reconstruction.

Linkage of the Ethiopia-Somalia dispute to rival Middle East formations risks escalation of the conflict by greater association with key issues in which the superpowers have an acknowledged stake. Arab involvement in the Horn of Africa may have the effect of heightening Israel's sense of isolation within the Middle East, thereby increasing its already profound dependence on the United States as a guarantor of its territorial sovereignty. At the same time, such linkage may also give the superpowers and the regional powers the opportunity to counsel restraint by both primary state actors. Some of Somalia's friends in the Arab world appear to have counseled against further escalation of the Ethiopia-Somalia dispute. There is, thus, no necessary relationship between expanded geographical overtones of the conflict and the possibilities of its escalation.

Superpowers. The two superpowers, the Soviet Union and the United States, constitute the fifth category of actors. Major European powers have never ceased to play an important role in influencing the relationships between Kenya and Somalia. Major European-power involvement has been a constant factor from the Anglo-Ethiopian treaty of 1897, through temporary colonial unification of the region under Italy during World War II, through British cession of additional territory to Ethiopia and restoration of part of Somaliland to Italy after World War II, to US and Soviet cold-war patronage of the rival powers ever since. Involvement of the major powers with Somalia and Ethiopia has had little or nothing to do with the border dispute per se and almost everything to do with their superimposition of rather poorly defined, shifting, but apparently conflicting interests upon regional relationships in the Horn.

Soviet and US policymakers have imputed strategic value to both countries primarily as gateways to influence in other diplomatic theaters rather than for their own sake. Ports on the Red Sea and the Gulf of Aden are relevant to oil shipping routes and politico-military competition on the Arabian peninsula, while those on the Indian Ocean have seemed valuable in that theater of Soviet-US competition. There is room to doubt, however, how far either the Soviet Union or the United States has found allies in the Horn of Africa critical to its respective global defense arrangements.

One of the larger and more populous countries in the region and the continent, and the home of the Organization of African Unity, Ethiopia is an influential actor among the African states despite its extreme poverty. The strengthened ties between the United States and the Arab world beginning in the Nixon years, together with displeasure at the course of the Ethiopian revolution, nevertheless caused the United States to deemphasize its commitment to Ethiopia after providing the country significant economic and military assistance as a regional cold-war ally for more than twenty years. Somalia dismissed its Soviet patron when the Soviets sought to replace conflict over national boundaries with amity between Ethiopia and Somalia on the basis of common adherence to scientific socialism. Somalia took advantage of an Ethiopia weakened by civil war as well as revolution to push its territorial claims militarily. The Soviet Union injected massive military assistance, over two billion dollars' worth, into Ethiopia to help it repulse the Somalis and also to contain the Eritrean insurgencies. The USSR has remained Ethiopia's dominant source of military assistance ever since, using that influence to encourage Ethiopia's evolution as a Marxist-Leninist state. Ethiopia's struggle to retain its present borders has weakened the country's ability to advance itself as a model Soviet-style, Soviet-inspired, socialist regime for other African states to emulate. To date, however, there is relatively little evidence to suggest that Ethiopia—with or without Soviet connivance—has sought to export its brand of socialism elsewhere on the continent, not least because the Mengistu government has been preoccupied with preserving the imperial boundaries by seeking to transform the empire itself into a progressive socialist order.

The Soviet Union has had limited success in its Ethiopian venture. By providing indispensable military assistance to Ethiopia at a time when the empire was crumbling, the Soviet Union enabled Ethiopia to sustain its existing border with Somalia and to regain a stalemate in Eritrea. Moscow thus helped the Mengistu government to preserve the empire, thereby helping it to accomplish its projected metamorphosis into a modern socialist state.

Ethiopia has responded by visibly gratifying the Soviet Union's apparent interests in the area, while covertly appearing to undercut them. The visible manifestations of a coincidence of Soviet and Ethiopian interests in the region have included: the establishment of a vanguard Workers' Party of Ethiopia patterned to a degree after the Soviet Communist party; support for the Soviet Union on Afghanistan; and observance of the 1984 boycott of the Olympic Games in the United States. More significantly, the Soviet Union may well exert influence on the Mengistu government for restraint in dealing with the Somali border issue. Beneath the surface, however, Ethiopian nationalism may remain a vital force. Let down by European powers on many occasions throughout its history, Ethiopia under Mengistu has taken steps to reduce the power within the government of those most closely aligned with the Soviet Union, while financing virtually all its economic development from Western sources, including humanitarian assistance for victims of the drought and ensuing famine.

The United States edged toward military support for Somalia in 1978–80, although only that which could be considered "defensive," in order to deter further Somali contravention of the OAU policy against redrawing colonial borders. At the same time, the United States began to increase markedly its military assistance to both the Sudan and Kenya, ostensibly because of the scale of Soviet military assistance to Ethiopia. By contrast with the cases of the Sudan and Kenya, the United States has moved very slowly to fulfill its commitment to Somalia because it has distrusted Somali intentions. Moreover, its appreciation of Somalia as a useful link in its chain of Indian Ocean defenses or as a steppingstone to strengthened relationships with moderate Arab regimes in the Middle East theater may have been only limited. US reticence in coming to Somalia's aid militarily appears to have influenced a changing Somali posture toward the Ogaden but at the price of considerable unhappiness within the Somali military. The United States has responded with infusions of military assistance, however, at those times when Ethiopia has appeared to be fomenting cross-border incursions into Somalia.

US objectives have been to check Soviet influence in Ethiopia, to sustain Somalia's capacity to resist Ethiopian invasion, and to encourage Somali conformity with OAU precepts on border sanctity. US policy may be only modestly effective in all three areas. Somalia's recent apparent acceptance of the WSLF's "independence" and its overtures to Kenya would appear to reflect a combination of postwar weariness with the Ogaden struggle, pressing internal difficulties diverting the attention of the Siad Barre government from regional initiatives, and

US pressure. Conversely, the Horn of Africa may be one theater where the Reagan administration's unilateralism[2] and globalism[3] may have been tempered by the recognition of regional realities. While increased US military aid to Kenya and the Sudan and the promise of the same to Somalia suggests preoccupation with the Soviet presence in Ethiopia, Somalia's isolated position within the continent may have caused the administration to encourage Somali regional accommodation. Significant in the same light is the restoration of humanitarian assistance to drought-stricken Ethiopia and its continuation in spite of charges of the diversion of aid to military uses.

Multilateral Management: Obstacles and Opportunities

The Ethiopia-Somalia dispute has not escalated, but rather appears to have been contained, at least in substantial measure, by the regional actors themselves. Moreover, despite the complexity of the situation and the fundamental issues involved, superpower confrontation over the Horn of Africa has not occurred. The exception is that in the context of deteriorating relationships between the United States and the Soviet Union since 1981, the Soviet presence in Ethiopia has frequently and uncritically been compared to the invasion of Afghanistan. The irony is that both the Soviet Union and the United States, on balance, appear to have acted with restraint to stabilize the Ethiopia-Somalia dispute. At the same time, under the doctrine of linkage, Soviet sins in the Horn have been taken as one additional justification for sharply reversing the US policy of détente with Moscow.

Multilateral involvement in resolving the multidimensional Ethiopia-Somalia conflict has been quiet rather than overt and highly publicized. Former United Nations Secretary General Kurt Waldheim was reported to have used the Libreville meeting of the Organization of African Unity in 1977 to seek negotiations between Somalia and Ethiopia when their border dispute heated up into open warfare. However, the very complexity, partial articulation, and interrelatedness of the issues appear to have prevented the United Nations from taking or being asked to take a more central role in managing or terminating the conflict. Somalia and Ethiopia complained about each other's behavior bitterly in the United Nations, but neither, according to the Secretary General, activated the formal mechanisms necessary to put the matter officially before the world organization.[4] Formal UN intervention was also impeded, from the UN point of view, because Somalia claimed that it was not involved at least initially in what it took as a secession movement of ethnic Somalis within Ethiopia. In short, the blurred distinction between international and domestic politics in the Horn impeded direct UN involvement in ending, limiting, or mediating the border dispute.

In the years preceding Somalia's independence, UN-sponsored arbitration of the border dispute failed because of disagreement over the terms of reference. The disagreement resulted from the confused definition of the border in the first place.[5] UN failure to resolve this conflict is, thus, part of an apparently declining record of successful conflict management since 1976.[6]

By contrast, the Organization of African Unity appears to have been a somewhat more effective venue for dealing with the Ethiopia-Somalia conflict. The Organization of African Unity's public posture, however, has contrasted with its utility as a quiet, informal venue for conflict management. The OAU has reaffirmed the applicability of its policy of eschewing border realignment to the Horn of Africa, thus favoring Ethiopia's position. The OAU has failed, however, to agree on strong conflict-management measures that in this case would give practical effect to such pronouncements. Informally and quietly, nevertheless, meetings of the OAU have provided opportunities for informal brokerage, while some OAU chairmen appear to have sought to serve as intermediaries. The OAU is, thus, given credit for helping to restrain the conflict.[7]

The United Nations has addressed the conflict indirectly in both geographic and functional terms. By promoting the concept of a Zone of Peace in the Indian Ocean, the world organization has sought to temper a larger, geographically adjacent conflict, which might both affect and be affected by the Horn of Africa issues. Similarly, UN peacekeeping efforts in the Middle East, however modest the achievements, have contributed to preventing patterns of escalation by spillover between adjacent theaters of conflict.

In functional terms, the United Nations and its affiliated agencies have concentrated on humanitarian and development problems that intensify the seriousness of the conflict more than on resolving the conflict itself. Hundreds of thousands of refugees, made more destitute by the Ethiopia-Somalia conflict, have streamed from Ethiopia into Somalia, Djibouti, and the Sudan. The Office of the United Nations High Commissioner for Refugees has established large refugee camps near the disputed borders. Most recently it has negotiated the limited repatriation to Ethiopia of some of these refugees. Other United Nations agencies, including the World Bank and the International Monetary Fund, have continued to bear major responsibility for development programs in both countries in an effort to prevent continuing regional strife from further retarding the achievement of improved standards of living in the area.

Disaggregation of Dimensions

A major thesis of this article has been that the regional actors themselves, with the apparent tolerance of and/or encouragement by the superpowers, have acted to contain, disaggregate, and bridge the multiple issues involved in the Ethiopia-Somalia dispute. One consequence of such regional diplomacy, should it continue, may be to isolate, clarify, and limit the root issue—the border dispute—and, thereby, render it more amenable to third-party brokerage. Such brokerage between Ethiopia and Somalia might then be more readily provided by a United Nations agency or alternatively by the OAU, a regional actor, or some combination thereof. The multidimensionality of the conflict continues, but disaggregation of these dimensions by diplomacy of the regional powers themselves may prepare the root border issue for mediation.

The Ethiopia-Somalia conflict has evolved within the broader context of deteriorating superpower relations. While large-scale arms transfers to the region by the superpowers have clearly not been caused solely by each other's presence in the region, the general climate of Soviet-US relations gives their military presence in the Horn additional and more ominous meaning. To the extent that regional powers are led to emphasize each other's military relationship to the superpowers rather than their regional relationships, trends toward constructive regional diplomacy may be short-circuited.

Lessons

The Ethiopia-Somalia dispute is but one among many. From a global perspective it is not necessarily one of the most important. Nevertheless, it is not unrelated to larger and more significant disputes. In geographical terms it adjoins and links two major theaters, the Middle East and the Indian Ocean. Major actors in the Middle Eastern theater have invested fairly heavily in the Horn of Africa theater. From this not unimportant conflict, therefore, what more general lessons may be suggested for multilateral management and resolution of international conflicts?

1. UN participation in the management of poorly articulated, closely interwoven multiple regional conflicts is hampered by conflict-resolution procedures that demand greater legal formality than any of the actors involved may think exists or is possible.

2. Despite the substantial presence of superpowers on "opposite" sides of the conflict during a period of poor superpower relations, the Horn of Africa appears to be a theater where superpowers have moderated rather than intensified the conflict. This is the case despite the passing of détente between the superpowers themselves.

3. The superpowers themselves do not appear to have any direct interest in the resolution of the Ethiopia-Somalia border dispute per se. It is the interrelationship of this and more fundamental regional issues that gives the Horn of Africa broader significance. The potential balkanization of the dominant power in the region, Ethiopia, and the participation of Middle Eastern states with actors contesting the future of Ethiopia are developments of sufficient moment to hold the attention of the superpowers. The interest of both powers, however, may be in stabilization as much as in seeking advantage over each other. At the same time, Ethiopia is a regional power of enough importance—its poverty notwithstanding—that how it sustains nationalism within artificial boundaries and what successful strategies, if any, it finds to promote development and improved standards of living will be widely noted on the continent. It does, therefore, hold "showcase" appeal for the superpowers and their rival systems.

4. The potential for escalation of the Horn of Africa conflict is present but dormant because of actions taken by the regional powers themselves to contain, disaggregate, and define the many dimensions of the conflict. Regional-power initiatives appear to be accepted and/or encouraged by the superpowers and, in any event, to moderate any tendencies toward superpower confrontation. Regional initiatives may also "prepare" the root conflict for mediation.

5. It is difficult to draw from one case general principles concerning the impact of external military intervention in regional theaters of conflict. We have suggested that the superpowers have in general behaved responsibly in the Horn of Africa despite global deterioration in their direct relationships. The merits of their arms transfers to the region is another and more difficult question. Ethiopia did seek Soviet military assistance in repelling Somali advances into Ethiopia during the 1977 war. Soviet and Cuban military assistance may well have been critical to preventing the balkanization of Ethiopia with its imponderable but probably substantial destabilizing effects on a larger region.

Promised US military assistance to Somalia may well have helped restore a balance of power and a return to the previous de facto Ethiopian-Somali borders. Delays in forwarding such assistance to Somalia may have contributed to a degree of Somali moderation on the incorporation of the Ogaden within its borders. US involvement with both Somalia and Kenya may have helped also to defuse tension between these two countries. On the other hand, US assistance to Somalia in conjunction with increased arms transfers to both the Sudan and Kenya gave Ethiopia justifiable cause to fear encirclement and may not have enhanced Kenya's efforts in particular to find a constructive middle course in the Horn of Africa conflict.

The tentative conclusion emerges, therefore, that while both super-powers may have acted fairly responsibly in political terms within the Horn, their military involvement per se was not based on a careful calculation of regional dynamics. The implications of this conclusion are: (a) superpower arms transfers should be tied more directly to their political objectives; (b) such political calculations should be based on sophisticated appreciation of regional dynamics; and (c) these calculations should include a full understanding of the diplomatic capabilities as well as the interests of important regional actors.

Notes

1. Tom J. Farer, *War Clouds in the Horn of Africa: The Widening Storm*, 2nd ed. (New York and Washington: Carnegie Endowment for International Peace, 1979).

2. J. Ravenhill and Donald Rothchild, "Reagan's New Unilateralism," 38 *International Journal* 1 (1983), pp. 107–128.

3. Henry Bienen, "Perspectives on Soviet Intervention in Africa," 95 *Political Science Quarterly* 1 (1980), pp. 29–43.

4. *UN Chronicle*, Vol. 44, No. 9 (Oct. 1977), p. 46.

5. Farer, op. cit.

6. Ernst Haas, "Regime Decay and Conflict Management in International Organizations, 1945–81," 37 *International Organizations* 2 (1983), pp. 189–245.

7. Ibid.

Bibliography

Arlinghaus, Bruce E., ed. *Arms for Africa*. Lexington, Mass.: Lexington Books, 1983.

Beinen, Henry. "Perspectives on Soviet Intervention in Africa." 95 *Political Science Quarterly* 1 (1980), pp. 29–43.

Brayton, A.A. "The Politics of Arms Limitation in Africa." 26 *African Studies Review* 1 (1983), pp. 73–91.

Brind, Harry. "Soviet Policy in the Horn of Africa." 60 *International Affairs* (GB) 1 (1983/4), pp. 75–97.

Bulhan, Hussein A. "Partition of Land and Pysche in Somali Society." 3 *Horn of Africa* 4 (1980/2), pp. 13–22.

Cassanelli, Lee. *The Shaping of Somali Society: Reconstructing The History of A Pastoral People*. Philadelphia: University of Pennsylvania Press, 1982.

Charlton, Roger. "Dehomogenizing the Study of African Politics: The Case of Inter-State Influences on Regime Formation and Change." 14 *Plural Societies* 1 (1983), pp. 32–49.

Chiteji, Frank. "Superpower Diplomacy: Arming Africa." *Current History* (Spring 1983), pp. 125–128, 138.

David, Stephen. "Realignment in the Horn: The Soviet Advantage." 4 *International Security* 2 (1979), pp. 69–91.

El-Kahwas, Mohamed A. "Foreign Involvement in the Ogaden War: The Arab Connection." Paper presented to the 1978 meetings of the African Studies Association, Baltimore.

Farer, Tom J. *War Clouds in the Horn of Africa: The Widening Storm*, 2nd ed. New York and Washington: Carnegie Endowment, 1979.

Geshekter, Charles L. "Socio-Economic Development in Somalia." 2 *Horn of Africa* 2 (1979), pp. 24–37.

Grabendorff, Wolf. "Cuba's Involvement in Africa." 22 *Journal of Inter-American Studies and World Affairs* 1 (1980), pp. 3–29.

Haas, E. "Regime Decay and Conflict Management in International Organizations, 1945–81." 37 *International Organization* 2 (1983), pp. 189–245.

International Institute for Strategic Studies. *The Military Balance 1983-4*. London: 1984.

Laitin, David. "The War in the Ogaden: Its Implications for Siyyad's Role in Somali History." Paper presented to 1978 meetings of the African Studies Association, Baltimore.

Lewis, I.M. *The Modern History of Somaliland*. New York: Praeger, 1965.

MacFarlane, S.N. "Intervention and Security in Africa." 60 *International Affairs* 8 (GB) 1 (1983/4), pp. 53–75.

MacKinda, S.M. "Conflict and Accommodation in the Horn of Africa: Kenya's Role in the Somali-Ethiopian Dispute." 37 *Australian Outlook* 1 (1983), pp. 34–40.

Markakis, John. "Material and Social Aspects of National Conflict in the Horn of Africa." 32-3 *Civilizations* 1-2 (1982-3), pp. 273–301.

Menon, Rajan. "The Soviet Union, The Arms Trade and the Third World." 34 *Soviet Studies* 3 (1982), pp. 377–396.

Ojo, Olusola. "Ethiopia's Foreign Policy Since the Revolution." 3 *Horn of Africa* 4 (1980/2), pp. 3–13.

Ravenhill, J., and Donald Rothchild. "Reagan's New Uni-lateralism." 38 *International Journal* 1 (1983), pp. 107–128.

Selassie, Berekhet H. "Conflict and Intervention in the Horn of Africa." *Monthly Review* (1980).

Skurnik, W.A.E. "Continuing Problems in Africa's Horn." *Current History* (March 1983), pp. 120–123, 137.

Stockholm International Peace Research Institute. *World Military Expenditure and Arms Production*. London: Taylor and Francis, 1983.

Thompson, V., and R. Adloff. *Djibouti and the Horn of Africa*. Stanford, California: Stanford University Press, 1968.

United States Arms Control and Disarmament Agency. *World Military Expenditures and Arms Transfers 1978-82*. Washington, DC: 1984.

Valenta, Jiri. "Soviet-Cuban Intervention in the Horn of Africa: Impact and Lessons." 11 *Journal of International Affairs* (GB) 2 (1977), pp. 353–367.

Young, A. "The United States and Africa: Victory for Diplomacy." 59 *Foreign Affairs* 3 (1980), pp. 648–667.

World Bank. *World Development Report 1984*. New York: Oxford University Press, 1984

PART THREE

Superpower Involvement

V

Afghanistan 1984:
Crisis After Crisis,
Internal and External

Louis Dupree

On the night of December 24, 1979, while shepherds watched over their flocks in the Hindu Kush foothills and the Turkestan plains, the Soviet Union began its invasion of Afghanistan, the first direct Soviet military aggression since World War II on an independent, nonaligned nation. Since that time, both the Soviet Union and the government of the Democratic Republic of Afghanistan (DRA) have insisted that only a "limited number" of Soviet troops entered Afghanistan at the "request" of the Afghans.

As of this writing, however, the Soviets have been fighting in Afghanistan for longer than they fought in World War II, and well over 100,000 Soviet troops are engaged in the country.

Some area specialists considered the invasion inevitable once the Soviet Union and the Eastern-bloc nations became the major development aid donors (loans and grants), the major military suppliers and trainers, and a major factor in the educational system. But the Afghans were able to maintain important balances in trade, aid, and educational programs with West European nations and the United States. In fact, the United States maintained a modest military assistance program with Afghanistan until the spring of 1979, mainly sending senior officers to advanced command and staff schools and junior officers for flight training.

Interventions are neither inevitable nor irreversible. However, once moving, they, like glaciers, tend to push ahead in a single direction

Louis Dupree is visiting senior research associate at the Islamic and Arabian Development Studies Center and visiting professor of anthropology and political science at Duke University. From 1959 to 1983 he was representative of the American Universities Field Staff, a consortium of twelve universities, in Afghanistan and Pakistan. He is also an adjunct professor at Penn State University. He is the author of the book *Afghanistan* (Princeton: Princeton University Press, 1980, first paperback edition) and a large number of articles on the area.

unless other interventions occur, with varying degrees of intensity and success.

Afghanistan before the Soviet invasion was typical of most preindustrial Afro-Asian nations, which were basically rural, agricultural-herding, multilingual societies. In such societies, regionally oriented kinship patterns, often tribally (i.e., territorially) oriented, replace government, in the sense that government (in the Western sense) revolves about groups of reciprocal, functioning sets of social, economic, and political rights and obligations. These reciprocal functions seldom exist between the governed and the government in the Afro-Asian region. The localized kin unit usually performs these functions.

In addition, the boundaries of the Afro-Asian region are all legacies of European imperialism, which usually split ethnolinguistic groups between separate national units and cut across geographic realities and ecological entities. These boundaries created problems of internal security as various ethnic groups sought out their relationships with newly established independent central governments. Problems of external security arise when common groups across boundaries seek to join together to form a single political unity, a new identity.

Therefore, any of these artificial boundaries can be changed, shifted, or abolished when a superior force is applied at a given place at a given time. When transborder violence occurs, all nations in the region are tempted to get involved. A number of such conflicts have occurred and still fester on the landscape: the Iran-Iraq war; the Arab-Israeli conflict; and Indian-Pakistani rivalries, which are partly responsible for the Bangladesh breakaway from Pakistan. All such regional disputes also tempt the superpowers to choose one side or the other to support, thus escalating the problems.

Possibly, the best way for the superpowers to handle these regional squabbles would be not to interfere and to let the antagonists solve their own problems, even if it means the two (or more) contestants fight. After all, boundary-hardening wars are actually nation-building exercises, just as those that Europe went through in the nineteenth century. However, success in isolating such regional conflicts assumes the superpowers would agree to remain outside the problem areas and send in no more weapons. Given the current state of the competition and mutual distrust generated by the United States and the Soviet Union since World War II, such a condition is highly improbable.

Afghanistan's past has been punctuated by warfare, both internal struggles and external interventions. The country is not unique in this respect, for all history has been dominated by warfare in various forms: actual combat, rumors of wars, preparations for wars, or the avoidance of wars, itself a form of warfare.

In the late eighteenth, nineteenth and early twentieth centuries, European imperialism intruded on the scene, which ultimately led to the drawing of the boundaries of modern Afghanistan by the British and the Czarist Russians. Afghanistan literally became a buffer state, separating these two great powers, so that at no point did British India touch Czarist Central Asia.[1]

During the hundred years from 1880 to 1979, Afghanistan was able to maintain a relatively balanced neutrality with occasional leanings toward one or another of the contemporary power blocs. Several important twentieth-century dates must be considered. The month-long Third Anglo-Afghan War was fought in May 1919 and resulted in the Afghans' gaining the right to conduct their own foreign affairs. Prior to 1919, Afghan foreign affairs were dominated by the British, under the Anglo-Russian Convention of 1907.[2] One of the first acts of the Afghan government of Amir Amanullah (1919–1929) was to recognize the Bolshevik regime, which returned the gesture. Although not always friendly, Afghan relations with the revolutionary regime (which in time founded the USSR) began early and lasted long.[3]

A tilt toward the British in India occurred after the 1929 civil war, which saw a distant cousin of Amanullah, Mohammad Nadir Khan, become King (1929–1933).[4] The Western tilt continued throughout the avuncular period (1933–1953) after the assassination of Nadir Shah in 1933, during which the uncles of the young Mohammad Zahir Shah (1933–1973) dominated the political processes.

The Afghans remained neutral in World War II, just as they had in World War I, but in the aftermath of the war, Afghanistan became involved in the cold-war competitions. After the mid–1950's, Afghanistan became what I call an "economic Korea," where the two superpowers, the United States and the Soviet Union, used economic and military assistance to win friends and influence governments.[5]

The leading Afghan figure during the period of cold-war competitions was Lieutenant General Mohammad Daoud Khan, a cousin and brother-in-law of the King, who seized power from his uncles in a bloodless 1953 coup. Many considered Daoud a Russian puppet, but in my opinion (and I knew Daoud well), he was an Afghan patriot, trying to maximize benefits for his country from the two superpowers. It turned out to be a dangerous game.[6]

A regional conflict over the status of the Pushtun (or Pathan, in many English sources) on the Pakistani side of the Durand Line of 1893 led to Daoud's downfall in 1963. The Durand Line has been a source of regional disputes several times in the post–World War II period. When the line was demarcated in 1893 (at times, very loosely on the ground), it split the Pushtun peoples, leaving half in the kingdom of Afghanistan

ABERYSTWYTH C.D.C.

and half in what evolved into the Tribal Areas and Settled Districts (North-West Frontier Province) of British India. Also, geography and ecology were unrealistically violated.

With independence, Pakistan inherited the British position along the frontier. The Afghans insisted that the Durand Line was not an international boundary and that therefore plebiscites should be held under international supervision to determine the wishes of the Pushtun, particularly those in the Tribal Areas. Newly independent India also became involved in the "Pushtunistan" issue and encouraged the Afghans to contest the Pakistani view. (The term "Pushtunistan" was invented by an Indian adviser to Kabul Radio.)

Although research into official documents and publications justify the Afghan view that the British did not consider the Durand Line an international boundary, the Pakistanis continued to stick to their position, primarily because the British had misled them into believing the line was an international boundary. However, the quote below from a British source is only one of many that can be found in the India Office Library and Files in London:

> "The Line was not described [in the 1983 treaty] as the boundary of India, but as the eastern and southern frontier of the Amir's [Abdur Rahman Khan] dominions, and as the limit of the respective spheres of influence of the two Governments, *the objective being the extension of British authority, and not that of the Indian frontier."* (Emphasis added. Classified *Military Report on Afghanistan,* published by the General Staff India, Government of India Press, 1925, page 69)

With the disappearance of Daoud from the political scene in 1963 (temporarily, as it turned out), a series of governments once again tilted toward the West, chiefly the United States, which was the major Western aid donor (grants and loans). Gradually, however, as the constitutional period (1963–73) developed, the United States became less and less interested in Afghanistan, partly because of commitments elsewhere, partly because of the belief that the Afghans would never "go Communist," partly because many believed the Soviets would not invade the country, and partly because Afghanistan was not considered strategically important.

The constitutional decade ended in chaos as the parliamentary experiment under a constitutional monarchy failed to make substantial strides toward socioeconomic and political development, in part because the Western-educated elitists appointed by the king could not break through generations of bureaucratic inertia. In addition, King Zahir, advised by conservative sycophants and members of the royal family, did not take steps either to implement the constitution or to suppress the growing opposition to the government's political lassitude.

The July 17, 1973, coup was led by former Prime Minister Daoud in association with certain Afghan military officers and bureaucrats, who, although trained partly in the USSR (and some in the US as well), were more nationalist than Soviet-oriented Communist. Most were members of the Parcham ("The Banner") branch of the leftist (socialist, Marxist)-oriented Jamiyat-i-Demokratiki-Khalq-i-Afghanistan (People's Democratic Party of Afghanistan—PDPA), led by Babrak Karmal. The other major branch, Khalq ("The Masses"), led by Nur Mohammad Taraki and Hafizullah Amin, preferred to sit out the coup. (The PDPA had been founded on January 1, 1965.)[7]

From July 17, 1973, to April 27, 1978, Daoud's new government (the Democratic Republic of Afghanistan) half-heartedly attempted several reforms in the social, political, and legal institutions. For example, the laws of Afghanistan were codified in four massive volumes. Land reform programs were drawn up but not implemented, and Daoud made a noble attempt to reform the bureaucracy, one of the major constraints to Afghan development.[8]

But after the promulgation of a new constitution in February 1977, Daoud reverted to being a classic tribal Khan and in March appointed a cabinet that consisted primarily of conservative sycophants, sons of sycophants, and even collateral members of the royal family. Also, by March 1975, President Daoud had succeeded in politically defanging his Parcham support by sending most of the young, enthusiastic cadre to the countryside, where they ran headlong into the rural power elites. These frustrated reformers either accepted the fact that change would have to be slow and consistent with existing cultural patterns to succeed or turned as corrupt as their predecessors. Others, also disillusioned, returned to Kabul and resigned—or were dismissed for leaving their posts without permission.

In response, the two leftist wings, Khalq and Parcham, remarried after a ten-year divorce, which had been brought about by personality and policy differences. Karmal of Parcham was a nationalist opportunist, who professed the desire to unite with all anti-monarchist groups to seize power. Taraki and Amin were also nationalist-oriented, but insisted on the primacy of the class struggle. Both groups had contacts with the Soviet Embassy, but, in my opinion, neither was dominated by the Soviets. The groups reunited in July 1977 in an obvious anti-government front.

A series of political assassinations and demonstrations led to the arrest of the leftist leadership and a subsequent, impromptu coup that bloodily overthrew the Daoud government and left Daoud and most of his family dead. The coup was led by some of the same military officers who had participated in Daoud's 1973 coup.

Much has been written, pro and con, about Soviet involvement in the 1973 and 1978 coups.[9] The best evidence suggests that the Soviets were not involved in plotting or executing either coup, but in all probability were informed that the coups would take place just before they occurred. If not informed, the Soviets may have immediately concluded that right-wing, anti-Soviet coups were under way, and possibly for this reason reacted as they did on December 24, 1979.

As usually happens after a successful coup, leftist or rightist, the two major party segments began a struggle for power. The military supported the Taraki-Amin faction, which initially prevailed. Taraki became President of the Revolutionary Council, Prime Minister of the Democratic Republic of Afghanistan, and General Secretary of the PDPA. The two main competitors for power, Amin and Karmal, became Deputy Prime Ministers, but this arrangement did not last long. Karmal and some of his chief lieutenants were exiled as ambassadors. The struggle between Khalq and Parcham continues, sometimes bloodily, as of this writing.

In August 1978, the DRA uncovered an anti-government plot and arrested a number of Parcham military officers and high-ranking civilian officials—in addition to several important nonpolitical individuals who were considered potential threats (at least ideologically) to the regime. Confessions were extracted from those arrested, and Karmal and Parcham were directly implicated. Karmal and other ambassadors were ordered home. Under the circumstances they declined, and disappeared into Eastern Europe and/or the USSR to serve as Soviet political soil banks.

Reforms and Rhetoric

As the Khalq regime preempted the leftist and/or nationalist position, it decreed a series of administrative procedures and far-reaching reforms. As presented, the reforms (land reforms, women's rights, abolition of the "bride price," etc.) ran counter to major Afghan social, cultural, and economic institutions.[10]

One of the first major mistakes of the new regime had been to arrest anyone remotely suspected of being a "potential" enemy of the state. This group included much of the nonpolitical intelligentsia, many of whom would have supported the DRA regime if given the opportunity— and if those in power had guaranteed the regime's independence of Soviet domination.

Too much was attempted too fast, without adequate preparation, qualified personnel, or a broad base of popular support. Some reforms contradicted others or even had internal inconsistencies. The most objectionable reforms and other DRA pronouncements were couched in Marxist-Leninist dialectic translated directly into Persian and Pashto. Furthermore, much of the rhetoric out of Soviet Central Asia was repeated over Radio Afghanistan. Therefore, the nonliterate rural population and many in the literate urban elite considered the new DRA Communist and Soviet-dominated.

It is interesting to note that the reform programs of the DRA were remarkably similar to most of those announced by Daoud's republic. But Daoud's government presented its programs in classical Dari (Afghan-Persian) and Pashto, and avoided Marxist-Leninist dialectic.

Revolts

Except for sporadic attacks by the Hizb-i-Islamic (Islamic party), a dissident Moslem revolutionary group with headquarters in Peshawar, Pakistan,[11] most of those in opposition to the DRA remained quiet until early fall 1978. However, periodic explosions, usually harmless, rocked Kabul, and opposition groups published anti-government tracts (called *Shaf-Namah*, "Evening News"). These incidents reminded the DRA that opposition to the regime did exist—and was growing.

Several factors account for the relative lack of early reaction against the DRA. The coup had come as a surprise, and most people in the urban centers were willing to give the regime a chance to succeed under its initially articulated guidelines.[12] Furthermore, and more important, spring and summer are months of major economic activities (farming, herding) in the countryside. Students of warfare often overlook, or underestimate, the relationship between leisure time and fighting in the annual cycle of preindustrial peoples. Even after preindustrial societies had contact with—and often were dominated by—technologically superior imperialists, warfare continued to play a major seasonal role in some of them, either as internal feuds or as yearly fights with the foreign occupiers.[13]

Intergroup and extra-group feuds perform a valuable positive function in preindustrial societies. Feuds during the off-agricultural, off-herding cycles help channel in-group fights over property rights and mate preferences into violence against neighboring groups, i.e., they serve to externalize internal aggressions. The blood feud functions to perpetuate one's own group, not to destroy other groups. Therefore, blood must be about equally spilled and properties (livestock and other movable objects) equally taken or destroyed. If one side gains materially at another's expense, the seasonal feud might extend into the farming or herding cycle—contrary to the interests of both sides.[14]

If, however, a central government goes beyond the bounds of cultural and political deviance, Afghan ethnolinguistic groups may unite locally to destroy local government offices and even to kill some civil officials (mainly tax collectors) and military or paramilitary (gendarmarie) personnel. But such attacks are usually a traditional way of expressing an opinion, and are not necessarily launched to overthrow the regime in power.

In early fall 1978, the regional revolts against the DRA began right on schedule, at the beginning of the economic slack season. The province of Buristan was the first to launch a traditional attack, quickly followed by Paktya, Badakhshan, Kapisa/Parwan, Uruzgan, Badghis, Balkh, Ghazni, Farah, and Herat. The DRA should have responded in the traditional way. Just enough government troops should have been sent into the field to stop the dissident movements, and then a Loya Jurqah (Great National Assembly) of regional power elites, religious leaders, high government officials (including military officers), and prominent intellectuals should have been organized to talk out the problems.

But a new factor had been added since the mid-1950's. The DRA had a Soviet-trained and equipped army and air force at its disposal, and the government overreacted—as have many third world central governments when faced with opposition from the countryside. Villages were bombed and napalmed and much blood was shed.

Government reprisals continued throughout the fall and winter of 1978–79, and revolts spread to every province in Afghanistan. As spring 1979 approached, large bodies of Afghan peasants and tribesmen did not return to their normal economic cycle, another culturally oriented signal to Kabul. Now the insurgents were fighting to overthrow. By late summer, Afghan military units (of the draftee army) began to desert in large numbers, usually with their weapons. The fighting had ceased to be a winter interlude, and the troops did not want to fight fellow Afghans.

The DRA government responded to the increasing pressures by requesting (and receiving) more Soviet military advisers and more sophisticated equipment. The Soviets did not want to be accused of deserting a new "socialist friend" in distress. By late 1979, most observers agreed that the DRA was in serious trouble and doubted that the regime could survive unless the Soviets directly intervened.

In late 1979, most of the insurgent leaders with headquarters in Peshawar sent forth the following message to the world via the BBC Overseas Service: "Our war is not with the Soviet peoples; our war is with the DRA regime in Kabul; and when the regime falls, we shall do nothing to disturb the 'special relationship' that Afghanistan has had with the USSR since the late 1950's." The "special relationship" had never been put into writing or even publicly articulated. But in essence it meant that the Afghan government never publicly went against the Soviet Union at international forums (such as the United Nations)— although the Afghans privately disagreed with the USSR from time to time. In return, the Afghans were free to accept aid and trade from nations wishing to engage in those two interlocking institutions and to send students to both East and West.

The Soviet Response

In December 1979, the Soviet Union apparently had only two viable options: to invade or not to invade. They chose to invade.[15]

Many scholars, including myself, did not believe the USSR would take such a step, mainly because it would establish a potentially dangerous precedent: it would be the first direct Soviet military aggression since World War II on an independent, nonaligned territory. Czechoslovakia and Hungary were not in the same category. They were considered by the North Atlantic Treaty Organization (NATO) and the rest of the world as already being parts of the Soviet bloc, regardless of what the Czechs and the Hungarians thought.

Probably, the Soviets planned a Dominican Republic-type operation:[16] eliminate the unreliable and unstable Khalqi government in power, replace it with a pliable puppet government under Karmal (Parcham), and leave within ninety days, having effectively extended their political control about 800 miles south of their Central Asian frontier.

Relatively speaking, only a small percentage of the Afghan population was actively engaged in resistance before the Soviet invasion. But the invasion triggered off another culturally oriented response. Many Afghan groups who were traditional enemies linked up to fight the invaders.

Afghan kin units (found in almost all areas of the country, but with varying modes of intensity) are based on vertically structured segmentary lineages (from nuclear family to extended family to lineage to sub-tribe to tribe), which are territorially neighbors to other lineages and which compete locally during the off-agricultural season, as discussed above. However, when an outside horizontal force threatens the vertical lineages, the tribes (or other ethnolinguistic units) unite locally to resist and, if possible, to throw out the invaders. Traditional enemies (such as the Mangal and Jadran Pushtun in Paktya, the Wardak Pushtun and Hazara in Ghazni, the Nuristani and Cujar in Kunar, etc.) united militarily to fight the Soviets, just as they did one hundred years ago to resist the British. Political unity may come later, growing out of military cooperation.[17]

The current situation most resembles the evolution of the Yugoslav partisan movement during World War II.[18] Initially, the seven major Yugoslav ethnolinguistic groups independently resisted the Germans and the Italians. As the war progressed, larger units evolved around basic political ideologies: the royalists under Draza Mihajlovic, and the leftists under Tito. Although the groups came together in politico-military elements, they never lost their ethnolinguistic identities. Out of these patterns emerged Tito's Yugoslav Socialist Federal Republic, comprising the socialist republics of Slovenia, Croatia, Bosnia and Hercegovina, Montenegro, Macedonia, and Serbia—which also includes two autonomous regions, Vojvodina and Kosovo.

Possibly, the present divided Afghan resistance elements will ultimately move toward the Yugoslav example. Local units could combine into multi-ethnic regional units and then link up, at a final phase, into a national liberation movement. But this may take a decade or two.

Why?

According to *Doonesbury* cartoonist Gary Trudeau, his Soviet UN spokesman, Viktor, confessed off the record: "We want to rule the world." I suspect the answer is a great deal more complex, but there are those who still find such reasoning sufficient. In discussing the "why" of the Soviet intervention, however, the following observations seem more pertinent.

1. Paranoia over security. According to all Kremlinologists, a major concern in Soviet foreign policy is the security of the borders of the USSR. This obsession dates back to the Allied intervention in north Russia and Siberia during and after World War I. (In fact, the last Japanese troops departed from east Siberia in 1926.)[19] Whenever the Soviets have been able to extend their frontier or influence beyond the Russian heartland with little danger to themselves, they have not hesitated to do so. The Afghan intervention, however, proved to be an expensive tactical minus, but, in the long run, may turn out to be a strategic plus.

2. US-USSR relations. Several actions and inactions of the Carter administration led the Soviets to believe that the United States would do nothing effective to counter an occupation of Afghanistan: the lack of effective American responses to the seizure of hostages in Iran and the burning of the US Embassy and several other US government buildings in Pakistan; the about-face on the "unacceptability" of a Soviet combat brigade in Cuba; the failure of the US Congress to ratify the Strategic Arms Limitation Talks treaty (SALT II), in spite of the Carter administration's support for it; the projected US-Chinese arms deal; the NATO agreement to upgrade the US nuclear arsenal in Western Europe;

the exclusion of the Soviet Union from the Middle East peace talks; the continued buildup by US naval forces in the Indian Ocean; and the establishment of Diego Garcia as a major military installation.[20]

In addition, the Soviet Union accused the United States, in association with Pakistan, China, Iran, Britain, Egypt, and Israel (this was the Camp David period), of sending men, arms, ammunition, and other supplies to the Afghan *mujahidin* (freedom fighters). This was at least partly true, but had basically no effect as the supplies did not have an impact on Soviet decisions concerning Afghanistan.

The Soviet military told their invading troops in December 1979 that they were going into Afghanistan to save a fellow "socialist" nation from the clutches of the "interventionists." The Carter administration reacted in a number of ways, mainly cosmetic. The United States refused to honor some of its wheat sales to the Soviet Union for the next two years, limited Soviet fishing in US waters, and cut back on the delivery of high-technology items in spite of several Soviet multimillion dollar contracts with US companies. (All the economic boycotts have subsequently been withdrawn, the final ones during the Reagan administration.)

Carter's boycotts hurt American farmers and businessmen. Argentina and other grain-producing countries helped alleviate Soviet shortages, and President Carter weakened his own sanction when he announced that the US grain exporters could sell non-US grains to the USSR.

The one sensible move—laughed at by some and criticized by others for introducing politics into sports—was the boycott of the 1980 Olympics. The Carter boycott, however, so disturbed the Soviets that they flew experts to Islamabad, Pakistan to put pressure on every Islamic country that attended the Extraordinary Session of the Islamic Foreign Ministers Conference (IFMC) in January 1980. These Soviet-country specialists argued, cajoled, and in some cases threatened delegates not to vote to condemn the Soviet invasion. When it became obvious that all the Islamic states (including the so-called Steadfastness Front of Libya, Syria, Algeria, South Yemen, and the Palestine Liberation Organization) would remain solidly behind the resolution, which demanded the immediate, unconditional withdrawal of Soviet troops from Afghanistan, the experts changed their tactics and pleaded with the delegates not to boycott the Olympics, which had become important political events to the Soviets as their winning athletes increasingly participated after World War II.[21]

3. Reaction to the Islamic political resurgence. The recent Islamic political awakening around the rimlands of the Soviet Union compounds the security syndrome. The Soviets feel that this resurgence might infect their Central Asian Moslems, who now constitute about 20 percent of the total population of the USSR. By the year 2000 (according to Soviet demographic projections), 53 percent of the total population of the USSR

will be non-Russian, and out of the total population, one-quarter to one-third will be Central Asian Moslems.[22]

The Soviets have not been completely successful in the "russification" of their Central Asian republics and have always feared that influences from the south (especially Turkey, Iran, and Afghanistan) would infiltrate across the border.[23] The Soviet Central Asians feel an affinity with the peoples to the south that is more cultural than exclusively religious. Pre-1979 Afghan exchange professors from Kabul University to Soviet Central Asian universities returned to Afghanistan with many tales of Central Asian Moslem envy for the freedom to practice Islam—but the Afghan professors emphasized that the affinity was always more cultural (and political) than religious.[24]

Also, it must be remembered that in two or three generations the Soviets have created a class of privileged bureaucrats in Soviet Central Asia, the bookkeepers of empire who are satisfied with their roles and statuses. So although few would predict violent responses to Soviet policies relating to their Central Asian Moslems, most view the invasion of Afghanistan as a Soviet warning to their own Moslems, as well as to the Turks, Iranians, Pakistanis, and Afghan *mujahidin*, that the Soviets will not tolerate Moslem-inspired internal dissent and external threats to stability.

But the lesson has not been completely absorbed. The original December 1979 invading force included large numbers of Central Asian Moslem reservists, called to active duty to fill out the divisions involved. Some estimates indicate that 30 percent or so of the Soviet troops were Central Asians.[25] Apparently the Soviets reasoned that the cultural Tajiks, Turkoman, Uzbek, etc. from Central Asia would have good rapport with their linguistic and cultural cousins in Afghanistan—and they were right. But the theory backfired.

The Central Asian troops (and other Soviet troops) found out that no "interventionists" existed, only Afghan freedom fighters. A few Soviets deserted to help train Afghan guerrillas. Some have actually engaged in combat against the Soviet Union. This is not to imply that large numbers have deserted—only an infinitesimal number of the 105,000 troops that initially occupied Afghanistan have done so. The friendly fraternization of Central Asian and Afghan Moslems caused the Soviets to withdraw most Moslem troops by the end of February 1980. Only translators and a few technical units remain. (In late summer–early fall 1984, evidence indicated that the Soviets had rapidly escalated their troop force level to 130,000—or even more.)

4. The Brezhnev Doctrine reaches China. When the Soviets decided to salvage the new socialist DRA, they effectively extended the Brezhnev

Doctrine to the borders of China, far beyond the region of original intent, with implications that reach worldwide.

5. The Warm Water War replaces the cold war. Did the Russians drive into Afghanistan to begin the final fulfillment of Peter the Great's dream—access to the Arabian Sea and the Indian Ocean—and to gain ultimate political domination of the region, now made more important by the oil of the Persian Gulf? On the other hand, in 1979 did the Russians really need to occupy Afghanistan (with Pakistan to come later) to have commercial outlets to the south? The answer is no, because before the invasion Soviet and East European goods flowed overland through friendly Afghanistan and Pakistan to India and elsewhere or reached the area through Indian and Pakistani ports via the Black Sea, the Dardanelles, and the Suez Canal.

In the military sense, the Soviet Asiatic Fleet could move additional task forces into the warm waters as easily as the Americans could. The Warm Water War has heated up since the Soviet invasion, and both superpowers have beefed up their naval and air strength in the region. And although the Soviets appear to have no hard-line plans to move to the southern warm waters, they will not pass up the opportunity if it presents itself with minimum risk, just as happened in Afghanistan.

6. Military pressures and professional advice. Scholars from nonaligned countries who were in Moscow at the time of the invasion believed that the Politburo asked for position papers from two prestigious Soviet institutes before making final decisions. The Institute for US and Canadian Studies was asked how the Americans would react if the Soviets went to the "rescue" of a "fellow socialist regime" in Afghanistan threatened by "bandit pressures" that were supported by "foreign interventionists." The Institute reasoned that the Americans would do nothing effective because the United States was at its lowest point in will, capability, and credibility since World War II.[26]

In addition, each successive American President since World War II has been tested at least once by the Soviets: the Berlin blockade, Korea, the Cuban missile crisis, Vietnam, Angola, Ethiopia, Yemen, Afghanistan, etc. At times, the confrontations were Soviet-inspired. Usually, however, the Soviets simply took advantage of an already-existing crisis to test US reactions.

According to some analysts, the Carter administration seldom appeared to have a cohesive, coherent foreign policy. A few examples of how the United States made policy during that period will suffice (not in chronological order and with no value judgments attached): the administration failed to support the Shah of Iran, then admitted him to the United States for medical treatment, and finally, invited him to leave; it supported Somoza in Nicaragua, then dropped him; it announced that a Russian combat brigade in Cuba was "unacceptable," then ignored it; it developed the neutron bomb, then decided against deploying it; it canceled a campaign promise to withdraw ground troops from Korea; it reversed the US vote on Security Council resolution 465; it failed to pass SALT II through Congress; it launched the abortive attempt to rescue the hostages in Iran; it imposed economic sanctions against Iran and harassed Iranian students in the United States; and it refused to permit Americans to travel to Iran. Successes were also tinged with controversy: the Panama Canal Treaty; the Camp David agreements; and increased normalization with the People's Republic of China at the expense of the Republic of China (Taiwan). No wonder Soviet specialists on the United States felt the Americans lacked will, capability, and most important, credibility.

Also, the Institute for the Study of the Peoples of Asia was asked what the Afghan people would do if the USSR came to the "rescue" of their country. The answer was that, given known Afghan historical and cultural patterns, the Afghans would resist.[27]

Both the institutes were correct in their assessments, but what tilted the Politburo in its decision to actually implement plans to invade? Soviet leader Leonid I. Brezhnev gave the official reasons in an interview published in *Pravda* on January 13, 1980: "The only task of the Soviet contingents is to assist the Afghans in repulsing the aggression from outside. They will all be withdrawn from Afghanistan once the reasons for the Afghan leadership's request for them disappears."

Probably it was the Soviet military that convinced the Politburo that it could end the insurrection in ninety days, place a puppet in power, leave behind a Praetorian Guard to protect him, and return home with the main forces, having effectively extended Soviet control to the borders of the Indo-Pakistani subcontinent—and having flanked Iran in the west. This proved to be a major tactical miscalculation, and the war grinds to the end of its sixth year on December 24, 1985.

Current Soviet tactics in Afghanistan involve the "rubblization" of the Afghan countryside (as bombers and helicopters attack defenseless mud villages) and migratory genocide. A dead Afghan is useless to the Soviets, but a live Afghan in fragile Pakistan or Iran may be a valuable pawn in the regional game of power.

About three million Afghan refugees live in Pakistan, and another two million or so live in Iran; every month the total increases. These refugees constitute about one-third of the pre-1978 15.5 million population estimate for Afghanistan.

Afghan refugees want to go home. But what will happen in another five years or so, when the refugees realize they cannot go home again? Will they become good Pakistani and Iranian citizens—or will they join fellow minority groups and possibly carve up Pakistan and Iran into independent democratic republics based on Islamic principles but politically guided by secular socialists?

Working through KHAD (the Afghan equivalent of the KGB), the Soviets have made substantial progress in penetrating Pushtun and Baluch dissidents (and possibly Sindhis)—as well as intellectual and student groups in Pakistan—and the Tudeh in Iran is still alive, though not so well. The Soviets did not invent or create these dissidents. They have been active since before World War II. Independent republics of Pushtunistan (Afghan and Pakistani Pushtun), Baluchistan (Afghan, Pakistani, and Iranian Baluch), and Sindhu-desh would isolate Pakistani Punjab and leave it very vulnerable to outside subversion. Also, most littoral nations of the Indian Ocean–Arabian Sea–Persian Gulf are politically fragile, with demands for regional autonomy evolving into national liberation movements.

International Responses

Currently, no acceptable regional power brokers exist. None of the countries bordering Afghanistan would be acceptable to negotiate a peaceful political solution, for each has enemies (or competitors) actively involved in the issues. China would certainly not be accepted by the Soviet Union; Pakistan and Iran are enjoined not to negotiate directly with the DRA by resolutions at various Moslem conferences; and India would be rejected by China and Pakistan—and probably by Iran.

What were the initial worldwide reactions to the Soviet invasion? As would be expected, it was universally condemned by the West, the Moslem world, China, and Japan. The Janata government of India, rapidly becoming a lame-duck administration, condemned the "aggression," but Indira Gandhi's new government, which took office in January 1980, began a course of waffling.

Not so expected, however, was the reaction of worldwide Communist parties. Some (Italian, Spanish, British, Japanese) actually condemned the invasion, as did many individual Communists and ex-Communists in France. Jean-Paul Sartre, for example, condemned the Soviet invasion and called for support of Carter's Olympic boycott. Fidel Castro, president of the nonaligned conference, was initially embarrassed, but ultimately recovered to support the invasion. Of the West European Communist parties, only the French supported the aggression. The US Communist party, led by Gus Hall, also expressed approval. Even more surprising, however, was the disapproval (if not actual condemnation) expressed by the Communist governments of Poland, Hungary, and Rumania.

The largely unsuccessful American boycotts have been discussed previously. Possibly, one of the main reasons for this lack of success was the failure of the Carter administration to discuss detailed plans in advance with allies and friends.

Condemnations by the United Nations General Assembly came quickly and have been sustained at a constant level over the years. Naturally, annual Security Council condemnations are vetoed by the Soviet Union and opposed by any of its satellites sitting temporarily on the Council. General Assembly votes over the years have been:

	For Condemnation	Against	Absent or Abstaining
January 1980	104	18	18
November 1980	111	22	12
November 1981	116	23	12
November 1982	114	21	13
November 1983	116	20	17
November 1984	119	20	14

The consistency of the voting patterns appears to indicate that the Afghanistan issue has evolved into a non-issue, resulting in a continuing moral condemnation on the part of most of the non-Communist world (and some Communist nations as well), with little or no action undertaken to solve the problem.

Probably, the most important early condemnation was the unanimous resolution of the Extraordinary Session of the Islamic Foreign Ministers Conference (mentioned earlier in the text) held in Islamabad on January 27–29, 1980. Even though President Carter chose this inopportune moment, while the Extraordinary Session was in progress, to ask the Security Council to endorse economic sanctions against Iran, the Islamic nations stood firm against the Soviet invasion. The resolution demanded the "immediate and unconditional withdrawal of all Soviet troops stationed on Afghani [sic—should have read Afghan, afghani is currency] territories," suspended the membership of Afghanistan in the Organization of Islamic Conference (OIC), invited OIC members to withhold recognition of the "illegal" regime in Afghanistan, asked OIC members to assist the Afghan refugees, asked all nations to stop aid and assistance to the DRA, called on OIC members to consider boycotting the Olympics unless the Soviets evacuated Afghanistan, and, finally, authorized the Secretary General of the OIC to find ways and means of implementing the resolution and to report to the 11th Regular Session to be held in Islamabad in May 1980.[28]

Subsequent OIC and Islamic foreign ministers' meetings have passed similar resolutions on the Soviet occupation of Afghanistan. Also, since the abortive attempt to rescue the hostages in April 1980, the United States has been strongly condemned at the same meetings for its actions against "Iranian territorial integrity."

The nonaligned movement meetings have issued milder condemnations of the presence of "foreign troops" in Afghanistan and have consistently repeated the four injunctions of the annual UN General Assembly resolutions:

1. a call for immediate and unconditional withdrawal of all "foreign troops" from Afghanistan;
2. a demand that Afghan refugees be permitted to return home with honor and complete amnesty;
3. an insistence that the Afghans have the right to determine their own system of government; and
4. a request that Afghan nonalignment, sovereignty, and territorial integrity be restored and guaranteed.

Noble goals, and the UN debates (especially those outside the formal sessions) indicated that the United States and the Soviet Union were expected to be the chief guarantors. Implementation has been negated by the continued Soviet occupation, which the Soviet Union and the DRA justify by allegations of "outside interference."

Some weapons have been reaching the *mujahidin* from the outside. This has been admitted by the United States and Egypt. Other countries have been involved: Saudi Arabia has given money; China has supplied weapons; and Pakistan has been the major conduit for both. The problem from the *mujahidin* point of view has been quantity and quality. The problem from the Pakistani point of view is protection of its territorial integrity. As of this writing, however, arms supply from the outside has not made a significant impact on Soviet operations inside Afghanistan.

Prompted by the Soviets, the DRA in April 1980 presented the world with several proposals to solve the problem of the escalating war. The government:

1. proposed bilateral talks between Afghanistan and Iran and between Afghanistan and Pakistan;
2. called for Afghan refugees to return home under political amnesty first announced on January 1, 1980 and periodically extended;
3. asked that the proposed bilateral talks have no preconditions;
4. stated that the "limited contingent of Soviet troops" would be withdrawn only if terms could be reached to "guarantee that

neither invasion nor any other form of interference in Afghanistan's internal affairs will be renewed" and that the nations concerned would eliminate the causes that made Afghanistan turn to the USSR with a request to bring the above-mentioned contingent into its territory;

5. demanded that the United States cease its buildup of armed forces in the Indian Ocean and the Persian Gulf (no mention was made of the Soviet buildup); and

6. suggested that Cuba (Castro was then president of the nonaligned movement) act as the go-between to lay the groundwork for the bilateral talks.

If implemented, the proposals would have created "normalization" in the region, which would have meant recognition of the Soviet-sponsored, Soviet-installed, Soviet-dominated regime of Karmal,[29] which was unacceptable to most non-Communist nations.

Beginning in 1981, numerous conferences have been held in Western Europe and the United States, all giving moral support to the *mujahidin* and asking for increased assistance for the refugees. Virtually all the conferences have supported one faction or another of the freedom fighter groups with headquarters in Peshawar. What has emerged from the conferences has been as follows: (1) Western supporters for the *mujahidin* have themselves been divided; (2) temporarily, the Afghan problem has stirred up world opinion, which subsided almost immediately after the demise of the individual conference; and (3) Afghans attending the conferences have tried to push their own views as to what had happened to Afghanistan before the invasion, what was happening, and what should happen in the future—and more divisions resulted.

Current Status

A political solution to the crises in the area appears impossible, given the current ingredients. Afghan resistance to the Soviet-DRA forces is stiffening, and urban guerrilla warfare intensifies. The Soviets have increased their force level and have escalated the war in several specific directions. They have instituted high-altitude carpet-bombing of villages and have increased the number and effectiveness of KHAD. The Soviet-DRA forces have stepped up cross-border raids into Pakistan, particularly whenever a Geneva conference is about to begin. All parties involved (including the *mujahidin*, the DRA, the Soviet Union, Iran, and Pakistan) have been unwilling to meet in direct negotiations, while external sources have increased the shipment of weapons and other supplies to the *mujahidin*, although not enough in quantity and quality to have an impact on Soviet policies.

The Soviet military apparently consider their losses in men and material acceptable—at this point in time. The Soviet public has evidenced little dissent over the war, either publicly or in the underground press, although there are some signs in the local Soviet media that queries about the war are increasing. Soviet state-controlled television occasionally features the war, exposing the atrocities of the Afghan *basmachi* (bandits) against their own people.

Contrapuntally playing through all the above are the successive UN-sponsored Geneva conferences,[30] inconclusive and unsatisfactory to those who want a quick and peaceful solution. Nevertheless, the participants in these conferences should meet periodically and continue the choreography of diplomacy as long as anyone will dance. The conferences offer a door waiting to be opened, when all parties are ready to talk peace, be it in 1986 or in the year 2006.

Under the guidelines agreed upon, no direct talks between the DRA and Pakistan took place, but the UN Secretary General's Personal Representative on Afghanistan, Diego Cordovez, held alternate sessions with the foreign ministers of Pakistan and the DRA. Cordovez acted as a diplomatic Ping-Pong ball, bouncing from one delegation to the other, reporting on the substance of the proposals and counterproposals of each. So far, no real progress has been made, but both parties agree that the United Nations' four points should serve as the basis for a political solution. How to implement the four points, however, has proved very elusive.

The main demands of the UN General Assembly resolutions include: the withdrawal of "foreign" troops from Afghanistan; the cessation of outside aid to freedom fighters and guarantees of no further intervention in Afghan internal affairs; the return of the refugees with honor; and the right of the Afghan people to choose a government system of their choice. In reality, the Geneva talks have bogged down over the issues of a withdrawal timetable and guarantees against future nonintervention.

The 1984 talks produced a "major breakthrough," according to the participants. "Proximity talks" were held for the first time, i.e., the Afghan and Pakistani foreign ministers were in the same building but in separate rooms, and not, as in previous talks, across town from each other. Iran was supposed to be party to the Geneva conferences, but has refused to participate until the Afghan *mujahidin* are represented at the talks.

One of the major tragedies as the Vietnam War wound down was the staging at the Paris peace talks: who would sit where, who would represent whom—even the shape of the tables was a subject of debate.

Now, however, the Geneva conferences have been institutionalized and continue to function. The door will, we hope, always be there.

The Continuing Crises

All nations bordering Afghanistan (Iran, Pakistan, even the Soviet Union and China)[31] have internal problems with their regionally oriented, ethnolinguistic groups. The problems are exacerbated because many of the groups slough over the boundaries left on the landscape as legacies of European imperialism.

A glance at the map of the Afro-Asian region will illustrate the problems left behind. Virtually no neighbors are friendly, partly because of boundary problems. Examples in the region under discussion are many, including Iran-Iraq (now fighting a war partly over the boundary in the Shatt al-Arab waterway), Iran-Afghanistan, Pakistan-Afghanistan, and Pakistan-India.

But regional fights are quite possibly the wave of the future, involving either the hardening of existing boundaries (a main Chinese policy since 1949) or the redrawing of boundaries into more realistic units. These wars will be nationalist-oriented, nation-building exercises like those in nineteenth-century Europe.

When the wars explode, however, the superpowers are drawn into the area and use the conflicts to try to spread their influences—if not actual control—or to deny control by each other. Of course that is why Afghanistan is unique; it has been physically occupied by an invading superpower force. Other nations have been invaded, but not by a superpower, e.g., Vietnam by China, Chad by Libya.

In Afghanistan, internal divisive tendencies continue, even though the Soviet-Afghan war rages unabated.[32] For example, when Soviet and DRA troops enter a region, former enemies often fight together until the Communists leave, and sometimes the old struggles for power break out anew. Meanwhile, the two factions of the PDPA, Parcham (supported by the Soviets) and Khalq, are still engaged in internal struggles, at times bloody, because many in the military are still Khalqi.

These tendencies are compounded by the fact that the six major *mujahidin* groupings with headquarters in Peshawar are in a constant state of political musical chairs.[33] Inside Afghanistan, local commanders are growing in strength, gradually stretching, if not actually cutting, the vital link to Peshawar. Contact with the Peshawar merry-go-round must be maintained, however, for the Peshawar parties are the major conduit for weapons.

In summary, therefore, the crises involve:

1. ethnolinguistic regionalism and demands for autonomy within federal political units;
2. incipient nationalism, which involves boundary hardening or changing boundaries left behind by imperialists; and
3. intervention by the superpowers when they perceive it to be in their interest—always in the name of peace, but in reality to continue their post–World War II competition for political and economic dominance of third world countries.

All these patterns will probably involve warfare, which is why the continued evolution of the Geneva conferences is crucial. As the *mujahidin* receive arms from the outside and the Soviets escalate the war, neither side appears likely to win.[34]

American reactions (other than those discussed in the text) have included the creation of the Rapid Deployment Force (RDF)—now a separate area command, the Central Command, to serve US interests in the Middle East and South Asia.

On the political scene, the US Senate, with the House of Representatives concurring unanimously, passed (97–0) on October 4, 1984, a resolution that called for the United States "to support effectively the Afghan people in their fight for freedom" and added, "it would be indefensible to provide enough aid to the freedom fighters to fight and die but not enough to advance their cause of freedom." In effect, the resolution tossed the ball into the court of the executive, which then had carte blanche (under the constraints imposed by the Senate committee that oversees intelligence activities) to escalate assistance to the freedom fighters. This was the first time in US legislative history that Congress openly voted to support a liberation movement.

Notes

1. Dupree, *Afghanistan*, 1st paperback ed. (Princeton: Princeton University Press, 1980); and V. Gregorian, *The Emergence of Modern Afghanistan* (Palo Alto: Stanford University Press, 1969).

2. M. Schinasi, *Afghanistan at the Beginning of the Twentieth Century* (Naples, Italy: Institute Universitario Orientale, Series Minor III, 1979).

3. L. Poullada, *Reform and Rebellion in Afghanistan, 1919–1929* (Ithaca: Cornell University Press, 1973); and R.T. Steward, *Fire in Afghanistan* (New York: Random House, 1973).

4. W. Fraser-Tytler, *Afghanistan*, 3rd ed. rev. by M. Gillett (London: Oxford University Press, 1963).

5. Dupree, "Afghanistan's 'Big Gamble': Part III," *Economic Competition in Afghanistan, American Universities Field Staff Reports, South Asia Series* 4(5) (1960).

6. A. Arnold, *Afghanistan: The Soviet Invasion in Perspective* (Stanford: Hoover Institution, 1981); and Dupree, *Afghanistan*, 1st paperback ed. (Princeton: Princeton University Press, 1980).

7. Arnold, *Afghanistan's Two Party Communism* (Stanford: Hoover Institution, 1983); Dupree, "Afghanistan in 1982: Still No Progress," *Asian Survey* 23(2) (1983), pp. 133–142; Dupree, "Afghanistan in 1983: And Still No Progress," *Asian Survey* 24(2) (1984), pp. 229–239; and F. Halliday, "Revolution in Afghanistan," *New Left Review* 112 (Nov.-Dec. 1978), pp. 3–44.

8. Dupree, "Toward Representative Government in Afghanistan: Parts I and II," *American Universities Field Staff Reports, Asia*, Nos. 1 and 16 (1978).

9. H. Bradsher, *Afghanistan and the Soviet Union* (Durham, North Carolina: Duke University Press, 1982); Dupree, "Afghanistan in 1982: Still No Progress," *Asian Survey* 23(2) (1983), pp. 133–142; Dupree, "Afghanistan in 1983: And Still No Progress," *Asian Survey* 24(2) (1984), pp. 229–239; Halliday, op. cit.; T. Hammond, *Red Flag Over Afghanistan* (Boulder, Colorado: Westview Press, 1984); and Poullada, "Afghanistan and the United States: The Crucial Years," *Middle East Journal* 35 (2) (1981), pp. 178–190.

10. Dupree, "Red Flag Over the Hindu Kush: Part IIIL," *Rhetoric and Reforms, Promises! Promises! American Universities Field Staff Reports, Asia*, No. 23 (1980).

11. Dupree, "Toward Representative Government in Afghanistan: Parts I and II," *American Universities Field Staff Reports, Asia*, Nos. 1 and 16 (1978). Hizb-i-Islamic was also mainly responsible for the abortive Panjsher insurrection against the Daoud regime in July 1975. The dissidents included some Setam-i-Milli. The insurrectionists came out of Bhutto's Pakistan.

12. Announced policies were: Islam; social justice under Islam; nonalignment in foreign policy; a commitment to the ideals of the United Nations (whatever that means now), and a commitment to honor all agreements made by previous Afghan regimes with foreign governments.

13. Dupree, "Afghan and British Military Tactics in the First Anglo-Afghan War (1838–1842)," *The Army Quarterly and Defense Journal* (UK) 107 920 (1977), pp. 214–221.

14. A. Ahmed and D. Hart (IIS.), *Islam in Tribal Societies* (London: Routledge and Kegan Paul, 1984); Dupree, "Militant Islam and Traditional Warfare in South Asia," *American Universities Field Staff Reports, Asia*, No. 21 (1980); and Dupree, "Tribal Warfare in Afghanistan and Pakistan," chapter in *Islam in Tribal Societies*, A. Ahmed and D. Hart, eds. (London: Routledge and Kegan Paul, 1984), pp. 226–288.

15. Several recent books have discussed the Soviet reasons, including: Arnold, *Afghanistan: The Soviet Invasion in Perspective* (Stanford: Hoover Institution, 1981); Bradsher, op. cit.; Hammond, op. cit.; E. Naby, "The Ethnic Factor in Soviet-Afghan Relations," *Asian Survey* 20(3) (1980), pp. 237–256; and A. Rubinstein, *Soviet Policy Toward Turkey, Iran and Afghanistan* (New York: Praeger, 1982).

16. A.F. Lowenthal, *The Dominican Intervention* (Cambridge: Harvard University Press, 1972).

17. M.N. Shahrani and R.L. Canfield, eds., *Revolution and Rebellions in Afghanistan: An Anthropological View* (Berkeley: Institute of International Studies, University of California, 1984).

18. Personal communications, mainly with Dennison Rusinow.

19. R. Goldhurst, *The Midnight War* (New York: McGraw-Hill, 1978); and J.A. White, *The Siberian Intervention* (Princeton: Princeton University Press, 1950).

20. Bradsher, op. cit.; and Hammond, op. cit.

21. Dupree, "Afghanistan in 1982: Still No Progress," *Asian Survey* 23(2) (1983), pp. 133–142; and Dupree, "Afghanistan in 1983: And Still No Progress," *Asian Survey* 24(2) (1984), pp. 229–239.

22. H.C. d'Encausse, *L'Empire eclate* (Paris: Flammiarion, 1978).

23. Naby, op. cit.

24. Dupree, "Islam: Design for Political Stability," *The Christian Science Monitor*, February 15, 1980.

25. Refer to footnote 9.

26. Personal communication.

27. Personal communication.

28. Dupree, "Afghanistan in 1982: Still No Progress," *Asian Survey* 23(2) (1983), pp. 133–142;

29. S. Harrison, "The Soviets Are Winning In Afghanistan," *The Washington Post*, May 13, 1984.

30. Geneva I (June 1982); Geneva II (April 11–20, 1983); Geneva III (or IIa, June 12–24, 1983); Geneva IV (August 24–29, 1984).

31. India does not have a common border with Afghanistan but is a potential "go-between." However, India is undergoing its most severe internal strains over demands from several groups for ethnolinguistic autonomy since independence in 1947. Also, India accuses Pakistan of supporting Sikh dissidents in the Punjab, a charge denied by Pakistan. So India would probably be unacceptable to both Pakistan and China—as well as to the Afghan *mujahidin*.

32. E. Giradet, "With the Resistance in Afghanistan," *The Christian Science Monitor*, June 22, 28; July 2, 7, 9, 19, 26, 1982. (Articles also published in 1983, 1984); Alan Guillo, Jean-Jose Puig, and Oliver Roy, "La guerre en Afghanistan: Modifications des Deplacements Traditionnels de Populations et Emergence de Nouveaux Types de Circulations," *Ethnologica Helvetica*, No. 7 (1983), pp. 139–153; J.J. Puig, "Voyage en Hazaradjat et au Pandjchir," *Les Nouvelles d' Afghanistan*, No. 17 (1984), pp. 15–16; and O. Roy, "Islam in the Afghan Resistance," chapter in *Religion in Communist Lands* (Keston, 1983).

33. The major groups are: Hizb-i-Islamic (Islamic party), led by Engineer Gulbuddin Hekmatyar, revolutionary Islam in the Khomenei mold, a mainly Pushtun following; Hizb-i-Islami (breakaway), led by Maulawi Mohammad Yunis Khalis, a traditionalist, tribal religious leader, support in Ningrahar Province, especially Surkhab region; Jamiat Islami (Islamic Society), led by Professor Burhanuddin Rabbani, revolutionary Islam, supported by non-Pushtun groups, such as Tajik, Uzbak in north, east, and northeast Afghanistan; Jabhai-yi-Nijat Melli (National Liberation Front), led by Sibgbratullah Mojadidi, a traditionalist faction from the Naqsbandi Sufi order plus south and east (Kandahar, Logar)

Durrani sub-tribes, including Popalizai, Karzai, Barakzai; Islami Melli Mahaz (National Islamic Front) of Pir Sayyid Ahmad Gailani, modernist, Pushtun support from Paktya, Paktika, Ghazni, Wardak; Harakat-i-Inqilabi Islami (Islamic Revolutionary Movement) of Maulavi Mohammad Mohammadi, wants status quo as of 1973, middle-of-the-road modernist, scattered support in north and southeast, mainly Pushtun; and Itehad-i-Islam-Baray-Azadi Afghanistan (Islamic Front to Liberate Afghanistan), led by Professor Abdul Rasul Sayyaf, traditionalist, small following, mainly religious scholars. Smaller breakaway groups (and splinters off from time to time) exist under such leaders as Maulana Nasrullah Mansur and Maulvi Mohammad Mohzar, both split from Islamic Revolutionary Movement, and Maulana Mohammad Mir, who separated from the National Liberation Front.

The ex-King, Mohammad Zahir, now living in exile in Italy, is occasionally mentioned by royalists and nonroyalists alike as the one person who could serve as a symbol to unite the various parties, both outside and inside Afghanistan. But quite possibly, intervention by the ex-King might be more divisive than cohesive. Many non-Durrani Pushtun leaders and almost all non-Pushtun leaders do not wish to see reminders of the old monarchy in their midst.

34. Groups inside Afghanistan not connected with the Peshawar parties compete (sometimes violently) for power. This is especially true among the Shia Hazara in central Afghanistan and the Nuristani in the eastern mountains.

VI

Grenada—An International Crisis in Multilateral Security

Michael W. Doyle

The invasion of Grenada on October 25, 1983, can be seen both as multilateral security's most striking recent success and as its most striking recent failure.[1] The Organization of Eastern Caribbean States (OECS) authorized with extraordinary decisiveness and planned with extraordinary rapidity an invasion to rescue Grenadian citizens from the consequences of a coup that they found intolerable. It rescued the Eastern Caribbean states from what they perceived to be a serious threat to their international security. At the same time, the invasion followed a period of confrontational US diplomacy that seemed unwilling to accommodate the previous Grenadian government (which the Grenadians had welcomed); it severely divided the United Nations community; and it revealed the failure of the United Nations, regional organizations, subregional organizations, and alliances with powers outside the region to meet the ongoing needs of Caribbean ministates for national security and political independence.

Hypothetically, a nation's security could be provided by national means (a national defense force), an alliance with another state (today, especially with a nuclear superpower), a regional or subregional multilateral institution (such as the Organization of American States [OAS] or the Organization of Eastern Caribbean States), or a global multilateral institution (the United Nations). Each has strengths and weaknesses; each has special requirements and likely results. Conventionally, multilateral security—whether regional or global—requires a shared and indivisible commitment to collective security among the members of the security organization. Ideally, then, the security organization is able to compensate for weak or unreliable national security or alliances by

Michael W. Doyle is associate professor of political science at Johns Hopkins University. His most recent book is *Empires* (Ithaca: Cornell University Press, 1986); he has written articles on a wide variety of international subjects.

bringing overwhelming and deterring force to bear against potential threats.[2]

The crisis in Grenada raises anew at least two perplexing questions about the meaning of security and particularly about the effectiveness of multilateral security in the context of today's international "market" for public security.[3] The first question concerns the roots and limits of escalation. How did a domestic upheaval in a very small island suddenly become the center of a major international crisis? Why didn't this crisis embroil the two superpowers? The second question concerns the proper scope of international security, especially when escalation is endemic. If national security is insufficient, can a ministate rely upon a superpower and yet preserve political independence? Can any level of multilateral security both be reliable and preserve the independence of its members? Can it be subregional? Must it be regional or global?

From Coup to Invasion to International Crisis

We still do not know the actual course of events surrounding the US invasion. But it appears that between October 12 and 14, the leaders of a coup in Grenada deposed and then arrested Maurice Bishop, Prime Minister of the People's Revolutionary Government (PRG), and installed Bernard Coard, Bishop's former deputy, as the new Prime Minister.[4] On October 19, soldiers from the Grenadian People's Revolutionary Army, in the course of a popular demonstration that had freed Bishop from house arrest, fired on the crowd—killing numerous civilians—and then executed Bishop, three of his former fellow ministers, and two trade union leaders. The next day, General Hudson Austin, commanding general of the People's Revolutionary Army, announced the formation of a Revolutionary Military Council (RMC) and imposed a shoot-on-sight curfew. Concurrently, a joint, armed intervention was planned at a hurried set of meetings among the United States, Barbados, Jamaica, and five states of the Organization of Eastern Caribbean States—Antigua and Barbuda, Dominica, St. Christopher-Nevis, St. Lucia, and St. Vincent and the Grenadines. (Montserrat, a British Crown Colony, participated in the deliberations and concurred in the invitation, but its actions were disavowed by Britain.) Consultations with Sir Paul Scoon, Grenada's Governor General, led to a request for help from him, according to Prime Minister J.M.G.M. Adams of Barbados, "well before" the invasion force landed in the early morning of Tuesday, October 25. (The request was confirmed by Sir Paul after soldiers of the invasion force freed him from the house arrest that the leaders of the coup had imposed.) By October 28, all significant resistance from elements of the People's Revolutionary Army and from the Cuban construction workers who were helping to build the controversial airport at Point Salines had been overcome. According to US sources, forty-five Grenadians (including twenty-four civilians), twenty-four Cubans, and nineteen Americans were killed in the invasion and its aftermath.[5]

The invasion of Grenada reached the agenda of the United Nations on October 25 as a request from Nicaragua for an urgent meeting of the Security Council. In three long and stormy sessions ending on October 28, the Security Council debated a draft resolution condemning the intervention as "a flagrant violation of international law" and calling for "an immediate cessation of intervention and an immediate withdrawal of the invading troops."

The OECS secretariat replied in a statement presented to the Security Council by St. Lucia. It argued that the invasion occurred under the provisions of Article 8 of the OECS Treaty, which obliged member states to come to each other's aid against external threats to their peace and security. The states of the Eastern Caribbean cited the serious threat to their security posed by the repressive military group then in Grenada that was acquiring control of the large military force that Grenada had built up. They feared also for the fate of the Grenadian people, as public order deteriorated. The OECS, requiring external assistance to compensate for the "relative lack of military resources" of its members, had called upon Barbados, Jamaica, and the United States for help.

The United States submitted a letter arguing that the intervention served the purposes ("human rights, democracy," US Ambassador to the United Nations Jeane J. Kirkpatrick later explained) that the United Nations was designed to promote and described the intervention's objectives: "They are to assist the Eastern Caribbean states as they join with the people of Grenada in restoring government and order, and to facilitate the departure of those U.S. citizens and other foreign nationals who wish to be evacuated. U.S. forces will work in close coordination with the OECS, and will remain only so long as their presence is required for those objectives."

Sixty-two speakers participated in a heated Council debate that evoked a widespread condemnation of the invasion as a violation of Article 2, paragraph 4 of the United Nations Charter, which obliges states to refrain from the threat or use of force in their international relations. At the end, the United States was forced into the unwelcome position of casting its veto to avoid being declared a flagrant violator of international law.

Three days later, on October 31, Nicaragua requested that the "situation in Grenada" be included as an additional item on the agenda of the General Assembly, then in session. On November 2, the General Assembly adopted resolution 38/7 (the Nicaraguan draft as amended) with 108 for, 9 against, and 27 abstentions. Voting with the United States in opposition were only its Caribbean allies in the invasion, El Salvador, and Israel. The third world bloc and the Soviet Union and its allies overwhelmingly voted for the resolution. All the Atlantic and Pacific allies of the United States abstained. Deploring the invasion as "a flagrant violation of international law," the resolution called for the "immediate cessation of armed intervention" and the "immediate withdrawal of foreign troops." It requested that "free elections be organized as rapidly as possible to enable the people of Grenada to choose its government democratically." It also requested that the UN Secretary General assess the situation and report back to the Assembly within seventy-two hours. At the same session, the Assembly strangely neglected an opportunity to establish a multilateral authority on Grenada. It postponed a draft resolution sponsored by the Bahamas and Trinidad and Tobago that proposed the immediate deployment of a Caribbean Community (CARICOM)/Commonwealth security force with the widest possible membership and "the immediate establishment of a broad-based civilian interim administration" to initiate arrangements for "free and fair" elections under international supervision.

The aftermath of the invasion revealed a less than settled Grenada. The General Assembly's fact-finding mission sent to Grenada was led by Under Secretary General for Special Political Affairs Diego Cordovez, who reported on November 6 that government buildings and Cuban residences had been destroyed by the invasion and that there was a complete absence of "political machinery for the performance of normal government functions." Yet Cordovez also observed that ten days after the armed intervention the marketplace was open and people were in the streets—"The major irritant for the population appeared to be the unofficial curfew," which the Governor General had requested the population to observe voluntarily. Sir Paul appointed an interim administration on November 9. US combat forces left the island on December 15, but the United States left behind 300 noncombat military personnel, who remained until June 1985. (Elements of a Caribbean Peacekeeping Force still remain as of October 1985.)

On December 3, 1984, the elections Sir Paul had promised at last took place, putting Herbert Blaize, a familiar and widely respected middle-class politician, in office. He and his party received 59 percent of the vote and fourteen of fifteen legislative seats. Despite evidence of considerable foreign funding in his electoral campaign, Blaize seemed to have the substantial support of the Grenadian electorate.[6] But whether his election will end the Grenadian crisis, bringing in a stable government acceptable to the people of Grenada, or merely renew it is a question that, given Grenada's history of domestic instability and international dependence, the elections alone will not decide.

The Roots of Escalation

The sources of escalation from a tragic domestic upheaval in Grenada to the international crisis that the country for a brief moment became lay in the dependence of Grenada on external political and economic forces, the desperate interdependence of the Eastern Caribbean states, and the dependence of the entire Caribbean region on outside powers, particularly the United States. The region has become a pawn in the ideological conflict between the United States and the Soviet Union. That the escalation of this crisis was limited and did not lead to a much more serious global confrontation seemed due to the minor strategic stakes involved for the Soviet Union and the tacit acceptance by the Soviet Union and other states that the Caribbean was within a zone of US hegemony.

Grenadian Dependence

With a population of 100,000, an area of 345 square kilometers, and a gross domestic product per capita of $930 (1983), Grenada's economic and political dependence on external forces has been a long-established fact. This does not mean that Grenadian events simply reflected outside pressures. After the country achieved independence in 1974, Grenada's politics were largely of its own creation. But in a domestic showdown, trumps always seemed to lie just over the horizon, waiting to be played by the domestic actor that reached them first.

Colonized by the French, Grenada was captured by Britain in 1762 and ruled throughout most of the nineteenth century under the strict Crown Colony form of government that placed the effective sovereignty of the island in the hands of a single colonial Governor and his bureaucratic subordinates. At the same time, sugar and spice plantations, together with all the evils of the plantation system, shaped an economy that exported agricultural products to distant metropoles and imported almost all its few capital and consumption goods.[7] A markedly skewed distribution of land, consumption, and power flowed from this pattern of development. As late as 1946, 103 estate owners (most of whom were white) owned 45.6 percent of the cultivated land. They, together with urban merchants and professionals (many of mixed race and immigrant origin), dominated the island's politics. The vast majority of black Grenadians were poor and powerless. But they were not subservient. They worked on the plantations and farmed small plots. Out of a total of 19,736 farmers, 18,456 tilled under ten acres each.[8] But ten acres was fully enough to support a family on Grenada's rich volcanic soil.

Britain established "responsible" (elected) government in 1951. But, according to the leading scholar of Grenadian politics, with both political and economic power out of the hands of the majority of the population, the island's political life took on an "irresponsible" character, reinforcing the dependence on and vulnerability of Grenada to foreign influences. Eric (later, Sir Eric) Gairy first took advantage of this aspect of electoral politics, becoming the "hero" playing to the real insecurities of the Grenadian "crowd."[9] Delighting in confronting and shocking the local "plantocracy" and the colonial Governor, he won the fervent loyalty of both the workers he organized in the Grenada Manual and Metal Workers Union and the voters he called into politics as followers of his Grenada United Labor Party (appropriately, GULP). He squandered public funds on his personal consumption at the same time as he established a "land for the landless" program by seizing a few of the remaining large estates (those of his active political opponents) and turning them over to Grenadian small farmers.

GULP held office from 1951 until its electoral defeat in 1957 by Gairy's middle-class opponents (the Grenada National Party—GNP), who then attempted to unify Grenada with the other West Indies—a plan that some observers consider was designed to contain radical populist forces. But the federation collapsed between 1958 and 1962. Following Gairy's next victory in the elections of 1961, Britain suspended the colonial constitution and dismissed Gairy on charges of corruption. The middle-class GNP then attempted another union—this time with Trinidad and Tobago. This latest effort to escape from the dangers of independence also failed when the Trinidadians, rich with oil reserves, balked at having to share them with their much poorer neighbor, Grenada. In 1967, Gairy returned to power and led Grenada through a constitutional crisis to independence in 1974 and into an increasingly bitter contest with the New JEWEL (Joint Endeavor for Welfare, Education, and Liberation) Movement (NJM).

Independence and the rise of the reformist and radical NJM did not end Grenadian dependence on outside influences. The economy remained dependent for its income on exporting nutmeg, bananas, and cocoa and on importing tourists. All essential industrial goods and petroleum (which generated all of Grenada's electricity) were imported. Independence itself, some commentators suggest, appealed to Gairy primarily as a means of expanding the range of international organizations from which he could solicit foreign aid.[10] Having enjoyed expanding exports and tourism in the 1960's, Grenada's economy, as did those of almost all the other West Indian islands, sustained a severe blow from the

1973–74 oil-price shock. And no sooner was recovery under way in the middle 1970's than the 1979 oil shock hit.[11] Gairy's regime also responded to opposition by looking overseas for political support, going so far as to acquire military aid and advisers from General Augusto Pinochet's government in Chile.

From 1973 through 1979, the economic crisis, the corruption of Gairy's rule, and the brutality of his Mongoose Gang (a public/private police unit) made Gairy increasingly unpopular and feared. Gairy's oppression also slowly built up the popular support of the NJM, a movement led by young lawyers, labor leaders, and teachers and inspired by the black-power movement and third world Marxism. The NJM's nearly bloodless coup on March 13, 1979 met with island-wide rejoicing. Although the Movement's forty-six-man army was domestically recruited, welcomed, and led, it too had found encouragement abroad. Cuban leader Fidel Castro had met with Bishop and the NJM leaders and promised them his support if their coup succeeded. The NJM reportedly had to purchase its guns in New Orleans on the international black market.[12] But Castro sent a security team to aid the NJM immediately following the successful coup.

The government established by the NJM—the People's Revolutionary Government—ruled from March 1979 until the coup of October 1983. During that period, external influences continued to play an important role in the life of the country. A straitened economy and pressures from the United States led to a desperate search for overseas sources of funds. Efficiency and ministerial honesty in the first years of the revolution enabled the government to live within its domestic resources for current expenditures. But all capital spending, including the large sums invested in the international airport at Point Salines, was met by foreign grants and loans. Harassed by the United States when it applied for funding at international organizations (see below), Grenada initially acquired most of its funds and supplies from Cuba and the Soviet bloc, the radical third world (Libya), and certain independents such as Venezuela and, later, the European Economic Community (EEC). Militarily and politically, the PRG leaned East, voting with the Soviets on the issue of the invasion of Afghanistan in the United Nations General Assembly and cooperating with Cuban delegations at international meetings of the nonaligned movement.[13]

The split between the two major factions in the NJM—those of Coard and Bishop—widened. The split was both a contest over who would rule and a choice of what direction the Grenadian revolution would take. On one side, Prime Minister Bishop, setting up the Alexander Commission to write a democratic constitution, promised the assembled leaders of the Caribbean that Grenada was moving toward electoral social democracy.[14] Bishop, the NJM's charismatic leader, probably felt that he could retain power under a democratic constitution. Internationally, Bishop favored authentic nonalignment. Although he felt a close personal tie to Castro, in the spring of 1983 he approached the United States seeking an accommodation. He was met with little more than renewed threats.[15] On the other side, Deputy Prime Minister Coard, identified by many as a hard-line Leninist and by some as a Stalinist, had acquired a reputation as a highly efficient administrator. He favored continued rule by the NJM vanguard. He had also established close ties to the Grenadian People's Revolutionary Army, to the Soviet Union, and, not so paradoxically, to the international business community.

When the Coard faction staged its domestic coup on October 14, 1983, all eyes looked overseas. The coup leaders looked to the Soviet Union and Cuba. The Soviets praised the Revolutionary Military Council headed by General Austin that took power after the murders of Bishop and his colleagues. But Castro denounced the murders and demanded that those responsible be brought to justice. Still, the Cuban construction workers remained, and there was no sign of Cuba's abandoning the RMC. Instead Colonel Pedro Tortolo Comas, an expert in managing factional disputes, was sent to Grenada, according to some reports, in order to engineer a counter-coup to put the revolution back on track.[16] At the same time, hundreds, perhaps thousands, of Grenadians were calling their relatives and friends throughout the Eastern Caribbean and the United States, pleading for some form of help. And the Governor General, according to evidence from those both supportive of and hostile to the subsequent intervention, established contact with Caribbean leaders and made known his wish for outside help.[17]

Caribbean Interdependence

Sir Paul's plea met a response that was already in motion. Soon after the coup on October 12–14, Prime Minister John Compton of St. Lucia contacted Prime Minister Adams of Barbados to express concern for the safety of the Grenadian people and the security of the states of the Eastern Caribbean. On October 19 and 20, Barbados and the states of the Organization of Eastern Caribbean States (absent Grenada) engaged in consultations. Contact with Jamaica and the United States with a view to a possible rescue mission had been established as early as October 19. On October 21, the OECS quarantined Grenada, voted for armed intervention according to the provisions of Article 8 (concerning collective defense against "external" attack), and requested the participation of regional and favorably inclined extra-regional military forces.

(The OECS had sounded out the United States, France, Canada, Venezuela, and Britain.) Previously, on October 20, the United States had diverted its Lebanon-bound task force to Grenadian waters. On October 22 and 23, at the request of Barbados and St. Lucia, the Caribbean Community, composed of all the Anglophonic states of the Caribbean, met to consider the crisis in Grenada. All but one of the members of CARICOM agreed to the following initiative:[18]

1. the immediate establishment of a broad-based civilian government of national reconciliation whose composition was acceptable to the Governor General. The primary function of that government would be the putting into place of arrangements for the holding of elections at the earliest possible date;
2. the acceptance of a fact-finding mission comprising eminent nationals of CARICOM states;
3. the putting into place of arrangements to ensure the safety of nationals of other countries in Grenada and/or their evacuation where desired; and
4. the acceptance of deployment in Grenada of a peacekeeping force comprising contingents contributed by CARICOM states.[19]

Sensing that they could not obtain the support of all of CARICOM for prompt military action should the RMC not accept these demands and fearing that accepting CARICOM negotiations would entangle them in endless delays, the OECS, Barbados, and Jamaica walked out of the meeting. These conservative democracies, particularly those closely neighboring Grenada in the Eastern Caribbean, were especially determined to rid themselves of what they saw as the brutal and ruthless regime then controlling Grenada.[20]

To account for their forceful and unprecedented reaction, we need to consider both the range of dangers that they saw in the new Grenadian regime and the special social, political, and strategic interdependence of the region.

The societies and polities of the Caribbean are thoroughly intertwined.[21] They are the "kith and kin" described by Eugenia Charles, Prime Minister of Dominica and chairperson of the OECS: "We, as part of the Organization of Eastern Caribbean States, realize that we are, of course, one region; we belong to each other; we are kith and kin. We all have members of our states living in Grenada. We are very concerned that this event might take place again."[22] In a speech before the United Nations Educational, Scientific and Cultural Organization, Reuben Harris, Education Minister of Antigua and Barbuda, summarized the extensive interdependence of the Eastern Caribbean states; he said that they are nations that enjoy "an economic community, a common currency, joint diplomatic representation, and responsibility for common defense and security."[23]

The elite from these many small islands have close contacts. They met in British educational institutions during colonial times; now they share a reliance on the University of the West Indies with its campuses in Jamaica, Barbados, and Trinidad and Tobago. The poor have relatives who have traveled far and wide in search of employment. New York, Toronto, and London have large Caribbean populations. Once, Britain, the United States, the Netherlands Antilles (because of the oil fields), and Panama drew large numbers of Caribbean nationals. Now the oil industry and economic boom conditions of Trinidad and Tobago draw thousands of immigrants, especially from the Eastern Caribbean. Crises such as that in Grenada thus send off an immediate and far-reaching wave of concern, often panic, as rumors fly and relatives call each other spreading word of calamity. Influential elites distributed across different governments are in continuous contact. Few secrets are kept, and at the same time, policy coordination rarely seems to depend on official channels.

Together, these factors help explain the nearly unanimous concern. But not all the states were prepared to support a military intervention. Belize and the Bahamas were too distant to experience fully the crisis of Grenada. Also, each had a desperate crisis of its own—the Guatemalans and crime, respectively. Guyana and Trinidad and Tobago had political reasons to avoid forceful measures. Guyana had recently been the object of a CARICOM investigation and censure for electoral corruption and thus could not have been eager to join what was beginning to appear to be a democratic crusade against autocratic oppression. George Chambers, Prime Minister of a democratic Trinidad and Tobago, rejected multinational action without official multilateral authority. He may also have feared domestic disruption—a parliamentary filibuster or a political demonstration—if the government supported an intervention. Trinidad enjoyed a degree of pluralism rare among the Caribbean democracies, having large Indian and Asian minorities, considerable differences in wealth, and a politically powerful, parliamentary opposition with close ties to the radical third world. (Only Jamaica matched its political diversity, but the opposition party of Michael Manley was in disarray after its heavy electoral defeat in October 1980.) Trinidad, the largest and wealthiest island of the Eastern Caribbean, also had little directly to fear from the Grenadian RMC. It may, in addition, have resented the prominence of its leading regional rival—Barbados—in the intervention.

The states that were willing to support military intervention had special reasons for such a response, in addition to the general concern for the welfare of the Grenadians. The OECS states, Barbados, and Jamaica were geographically near and, as conservative capitalist democracies, were deeply hostile to the "Stalinist" militarism they saw in the RMC. Their relations with Grenada under the NJM's rule had oscillated from welcome, following the ouster of the widely despised Gairy regime, to hostility, as the NJM threatened Caribbean-wide revolution and delayed implementing its promises of elections, to tolerance, as Bishop's government tempered its revolutionary rhetoric in 1982 and announced in 1983 the formation of an electoral commission. The coup and the vicious killings created extreme revulsion among the informed public; it soon became widely reported that Jacqueline Creft, the former Minister of Education in the PRG who was pregnant with Bishop's child, had been beaten to death by the soldiers during the massacre of October 19.[24] In addition to being an unprecedented outbreak of violence for the Commonwealth Caribbean, these killings seemed to validate those states' most extreme fears of Communist tyranny and aggression.

Their fears were exacerbated by the proximity and the military vulnerability of the ministates of the Eastern Caribbean. Grenada's People's Revolutionary Army was composed of a regular force of 1,000 persons and a militia of two to three times that number. And it possessed uniforms and automatic rifles for a force of 10,000 persons, armored vehicles, howitzers, and coastal patrol boats. The states of the Eastern Caribbean combined possessed defense forces (glorified policemen) totaling 500, with no heavy weaponry. None of the states of the OECS was or is vulnerable to the sort of forty-six-man invasion-coup that toppled Gairy's regime. But each state harbored small, potentially aggressive groups, which, if armed or supported by external force, could cause severe disruption, loss of life, and expense before they were eventually arrested. Communications on some of the islands were so inadequate that news of an invasion would first reach the capital by word of mouth.[25]

The governments of the OECS were thus determined to rid themselves of their dangerous new neighbor. They justified this action as a measure pursuant to their treaty of common security to which Grenada was a party. None of these states, however, singly or together, had the forces to oust the RMC from Grenada. Barbados and Jamaica, though better armed than the states of the OECS, lacked the minimal military superiority (three to one), not to speak of the transportation and logistics, that an interventionary force required. When CARICOM refused to endorse a prompt intervention, they fell back on their eager partner, the United States, which was more than willing and able to supply the forces they lacked.

United States Policy—Confrontation, Cold or Hot

The United States did not merely respond to a Caribbean request for help; it had its own concerns that were parallel, although not identical, to those of the Caribbean. The official State Department position as enunciated by Deputy Secretary of State Kenneth Dam cited two concerns: to protect the lives of US citizens and to help Grenada reestablish law and order, following the requests from the OECS and the Grenadian Governor General.[26]

Planning for a "nonpermissive evacuation" of US citizens began as early as October 15, as news of the crisis in Grenada reached Washington. The events of the following week escalated the planning. As the difficulty of a forcible rescue of US citizens (the students from the American Medical School at St. Georges and the homeowners scattered across the island) became apparent, planning turned to a full-scale intervention to oust the RMC. Plans were developed in conjunction with the OECS. The diversion of the Lebanon task force and the mobilization of the US Army Rangers and elements of the Rapid Deployment Force brought the requisite military force within reach.

First, however, the United States sent envoys to Grenada to determine whether the RMC would permit an evacuation of American citizens. The envoys reported that the RMC appeared to be stalling, either purposefully or because it was losing control of a disintegrating political situation.[27] The RMC would permit standard departures, going through customs, etc., but not a special evacuation by ship or air. (Standard exit procedures, we can surmise, would have avoided further arousing Grenadian citizens and would have placed pressure on the OECS and CARICOM to lift their quarantine of Grenada.) Out of the approximately 1,000 residents and medical students, the consular envoys reached 300 US citizens, who signed a petition requesting a special exit.[28] President Ronald Reagan gave the final go-ahead for the planned invasion after learning of the RMC's refusal to provide special measures for the evacuation of US citizens.

The bombing of the marines in Lebanon during the weekend that the Grenada crisis peaked recalled the political disaster President Jimmy Carter had suffered over the seizure of the US hostages in Iran in 1979. President Reagan, facing a disaster in Lebanon and a looming replay of the hostage crisis in Grenada, was heard to lament, "I'm no better off than Jimmy Carter."[29] Nonetheless, US attention to Grenada did not begin with the coup of October 12–14. Indeed, in light of the economic and psychological warfare the United States had been waging against Grenada since its 1979 revolution, the coup, the OECS request, and the potential threat to US residents appear more as the occasions, or the excuses, for an outcome—the crushing of Grenada's People's Revolutionary Government—that was long desired and even, apparently, planned.

President Reagan's initial justifications for the invasion gave some sense of what had been driving American policy toward Grenada since March 1979. Then he had emphasized the Cuban-Soviet military presence as much as the rescue of US citizens. Grenada, he announced, "was a Soviet-Cuban colony being readied as a major military bastion to export terrorism and undermine democracy."[30]

On March 23, 1983, the President identified what his administration thought to be the dual threat that Grenada posed. The airport at Point Salines was, he charged, a military installation, a "power projection" being built by the Cubans "with Soviet financing." This militarization of Grenada threatened US national security by putting at risk US geo-economic and geostrategic interests in the Caribbean, "a very important passageway for our international commerce and military lines of communication. More than half of American oil imports now pass through the Caribbean."[31] The second threat was the ideological advance of communism. Secretary of State George P. Shultz amplified, "As Grenada demonstrated, we must defend ourselves against the organized violence of Communism."[32] And in explaining his policy of "restoring deterrence," President Reagan indicated the sort of events he proposed to deter: "The simple fact is that in the late 1970's we were not deterring, as events in Angola and Afghanistan made clear."[33]

These goals, of course, were not new. Collaborating with Britain and later replacing it, the United States has attempted to maintain imperial or hegemonic control of its Caribbean "American backyard" since the Spanish-American War. It has waged a cold war against Communism during the entire postwar period.[34] But President Reagan's cold war in the Caribbean followed a period in the 1970's that had been noticeable for a lull in tension. In the late 1960's, efforts to assassinate Castro appear to have been curtailed. The Nixon Doctrine emphasized regionalism—the devolution of security to regional actors. Then the Carter administration negotiated a historic settlement of the Panama Canal, attempted to negotiate a détente with Cuba, distanced itself, on human rights grounds, from the military dictators who had been traditional US allies, and decided to tolerate the Nicaraguan revolution. Together, these initiatives suggested to many that the United States was relaxing its interventionism.

The March 1979 coup led by Bishop in Grenada was met with a parallel initial tolerance. The United States offered surplus regional aid funds to the strapped revolutionary government. (Unfortunately, the Grenadians perceived the sum, $5,000, as insulting and denounced American imperialism.) But soon, under pressure of the debacle in Iran, the Soviet "combat brigade" in Cuba, and a supposed Caribbean "circle of crisis," the Carter administration began economically and politically to quarantine Grenada, refusing, for example, to permit it to share in funds allocated for a program that was designed to help the region recover from Hurricane David. The National Security Council also, it is reported, considered but rejected a blockade of Grenada in the spring of 1980.[35]

The Reagan administration on assuming office radically escalated the economic and military confrontation with Grenada's People's Revolutionary Government. President Reagan cut off all American aid in March 1981 and urged the European Economic Community to deny Grenada a grant for its international airport. This airport was the centerpiece of the PRG's plan for economic development and was designed to stimulate its tourist trade. The United States said the airport was uneconomic and planned for Soviet-Cuban military use, although Washington has not made available evidence indicating that the airport was being prepared for military use. Any airport suited for intercontinental jets, apparently, can be readily converted into a military air base. But the British contractor (Plessey and Company) working on the airport said it observed no specifically military construction. One can speculate that even a civilian international airport in Grenada would improve the airlift capacity of Cuba, reducing its costs and current dependence on the Soviet Union for the transport of men and matériel to Africa. After the airport was modified, it could serve in addition as a convenient base for extending Soviet air reconnaissance. But as the only airfield available to Cuba or the Soviet Union in the southern Caribbean, it would also make whatever air forces were stationed there extremely vulnerable in a crisis to US interdiction or sabotage. Despite US efforts to cut off funds, the airport received matériel and financing from the Cubans, the Libyans, the Venezuelans, and later the Europeans and others. It is now being completed—only for tourists, according to the administration—with aid from the United States.

In April 1981, the administration also lobbied against an International Monetary Fund (IMF) loan that was supported on financial grounds by the director of the IMF, and in July of the same year attempted to stipulate that a $4 million loan to the Caribbean Development Bank, of which Grenada is a full member, not be used in any part to fund loans to Grenada. (The Caribbean Development Bank declined the loan under those conditions.)

Military intimidation, too, played a part in American strategy. In August 1981, a huge armada, the largest assembled since World War II, churned the waters about Cuba. It also carried a none-too-subtle message for Grenada, for it included an amphibious landing on the island of

Vieques (off Puerto Rico), code-named Amber, directed against "Amber and the Amberdines." Alarmed Grenadian officials noted the similarity to the names Grenada and the Grenadines—the latter being a string of small islands off the coast of Grenada. They also remarked that the landing exercise included a simultaneous attack on two airports, suggestive of Grenada's two airports, one of which, moreover—the controversial one being built with Cuban aid at Point Salines—is adjacent to a district called Amber. In the spring of 1983, the CIA, apparently speaking for the administration, reportedly proposed a plan to destabilize Grenada; but the proposal was rejected by the Senate Intelligence Oversight Committee.[36]

When in June 1983 Prime Minister Bishop announced the formation of an electoral commission and visited the United States trying to avert the mounting confrontation, he met with Deputy Secretary of State Dam and national security adviser William Clark. From the Deputy Secretary, Bishop received assurances that the United States would tolerate Grenada if it steered clear of a direct alliance with the Soviet bloc. From Clark, on the other hand, Bishop received threats of further restrictions on tourist travel and the withdrawal of the American Medical School at St. Georges, an important local source of revenue, unless Grenada agreed to change its form of government and to adopt policies in line with those of the United States.[37] While the United States' embracing Bishop might well have hastened his fall, coercing him— narrowing his options—played into the hands of Coard and the military within Grenada, who were determined to hold the island on an authoritarian and pro-Soviet path. The stage was now set for the domestic crisis and the international intervention that engulfed Grenada in October.

The Grenadian crisis thus escalated when the Governor General and the mass of the Grenadians refused to accept the coup, when the Organization of Eastern Caribbean States, Jamaica, and Barbados refused to accept the delay that negotiating with the RMC would involve, and when an eager US partner with both reasons of its own and the military force to oust the RMC volunteered its services. But the escalation did not proceed further, Cuba and the Soviet Union choosing not to become more involved. Cuba had little inclination, it appears, to support the RMC and condemned the coup in the strongest possible terms. The Soviets may have had little wish to escalate for such small stakes, and in any case they had few resources to bring to bear in the area without Cuban support and with the very little time left them by the speed of the OECS-US response. And after the arrest of the leaders of the Coard-Austin faction, it would have been next to impossible for the Soviet Union to find Soviet supporters left on the island for the USSR to sustain.

A Success and a Failure

Despite the "success in a multilateral mode" hailed by US Assistant Secretary of State for Inter-American Affairs Langhorne Motley,[38] the Grenada invasion was an ad hoc multinational[39] operation endorsed by a multilateral organization and enforced by the United States. Its success was at best mixed. The closer one was, geographically, to the actual intervention, the more successful it appeared. The farther away, the worse it seemed.

To the people of Grenada, the invasion by almost all reports was a rescue. In one poll taken soon after the invasion, 91 percent welcomed the toppling of the coup by US and Caribbean forces.[40] In a scientifically conducted poll taken in December 1983 and January 1984, 86 percent welcomed the multinational operation as "a good thing."[41] (Grenada appears to have been the first locally popular invasion, overt or covert, that the United States has mounted since the Battle of Normandy on D Day.)

The older generation of Grenadians had tolerated the NJM's "revolution." But the coup, the Revolutionary Military Council, the shoot-on-sight curfew, and the rounding up of the leading supporters of Bishop realized their worst fears. The mass of young supporters of the NJM, including the thousands of school students who freed Bishop on October 19, saw the slaughter of the Bishop Cabinet as signaling the death of the populist reform movement that they had supported. "No Bish, No Revo," their signs said. To the Grenadians, it appears, the prospect of continued rule by the hard-line party and military faction was simply worse than a foreign rescue—even though a rescue meant an invasion.

To most of the states of the Eastern Caribbean, the intervention removed what they thought to be a serious security threat and an unprecedentedly vicious regime. They were prepared to have US and other foreign forces intervene in their region as the only effective resort: "We don't have the capacity, ourselves," Charles explained, "to see to it that the Grenadians get the freedom they're required to have to choose their own government."[42] And no alternative to invasion seemed to them to be more effective and less dangerous to innocent lives. Grenada's Revolutionary Military Council had neither taken steps to punish those responsible for the killings of October nor even expressed regret. Yet it appeared to have retained the allegiance of the regular army and thus the capacity to crush another public uprising. These states therefore rejected Trinidad and Tobago's plan for a CARICOM solution because they suspected that delay would only allow the RMC to entrench itself further and that in the end CARICOM lacked the forces to remove the RMC.[43]

Participants at the meetings at which the OECS, the United States, Jamaica, and Barbados planned the invasion can recall no consideration of bringing the crisis to either the Organization of American States or the United Nations. This they explain by the Caribbean alienation from the OAS (seen as a Latin institution hostile to black and Anglophonic Caribbean states) and the perception by Eastern Caribbean leaders that the United Nations was incapable of either rapid or effective action.[44] The leaders of the Caribbean regret the split that has developed between the invasion's supporters and its two leading opponents, Trinidad and Tobago and Guyana. They resent the condemnation they suffered in the United Nations by the votes of the third world, although this rift was partly repaired shortly thereafter at the November 24 meeting of the Commonwealth in New Delhi, which decided not to condemn the OECS states. But support for the invasion among the governments and the mass of the people of the region has yet to wane.

To many in the Reagan administration, the invasion was reportedly a success that avoided "another Iran" (another hostage crisis), "another Beirut" (where the United States appeared helpless), and "another Nicaragua" (another "outpost" for Cuba and the Soviet Union).[45] On the day after the General Assembly resolution condemning the invasion as a flagrant violation of international law, President Reagan announced that the condemnation "didn't disturb my breakfast at all."[46] Eliminating the possibility of a strategic "hostile triangle" in the Caribbean (Cuba, Nicaragua, and Grenada) had long been an administration aim. But it appears to have been the potential-hostage issue that the administration employed to win the support of 63 percent of the public (its highest approval rating in the preceding two years) and to rout its Democratic critics.[47]

Given the anti-interventionist leanings of most of the American public, this was a surprising result. The public's endorsement of the Grenada invasion—a domestic coup in public opinion by the President—seems to have resulted from an adroit coalition of indirect mass public support, direct (but minority) support, neutralized opposition, and confusion.

Public opinion in the United States tends to divide into two groups. Approximately half the electorate—the mass, or inattentive, public—are "noninternationalist." They believe in "peace" and "strength" (national security), rejecting both international cooperation (foreign aid) and international intervention. The attentive public is "internationalist," but is divided into liberal internationalists—who advocate détente, international cooperation, human rights, and nonintervention—and conservative internationalists, who advocate anticommunism, military strength, human rights, and intervention.[48]

In 1980, President Reagan took advantage of a growing public sentiment in favor of a strengthened defense to unite behind his election the concern for strength of the mass public with the commitment to anticommunism of the conservative internationalists. But inconclusive meddling by the United States in the crises in Poland, El Salvador, the Falkland Islands (Malvinas), and Lebanon eroded Reagan's support among the public on foreign policy issues. The mass public seemed to judge that the defense buildup was now sufficient and that the President was becoming dangerously interventionist.[49]

The surge of support for the Grenada intervention in part reflects the boost a president receives during any crisis. But unlike Lebanon, public support held in Grenada largely, it appears, because Grenada was regarded not as an intervention issue but as a strength issue. The rapid military success of the operation averted an anti-war backlash from the mass public. Rescuing American citizens from "foreign danger"—an event celebrated on TV by the returning medical students—demonstrated strength.

For the attentive, internationalist public, other factors seem to have been at work. Conservative internationalists may simply have regarded the invasion as a successful stroke against the extension of Communism. Indeed, the President's own history of referring to Grenada as a "Cuban-Soviet colony" responded to this set of concerns. At the same time, leading liberal internationalists found themselves in a difficult position, at first vehemently denouncing and then accepting the "legitimacy" of the invasion.

Liberal congressmen and most of the liberal public eventually chose to accept the potential-hostage justification for the invasion. Nonetheless, Congressman Don Bonker, a member of the Foley delegation sent by Speaker of the House of Representatives Thomas P. (Tip) O'Neill, Jr., to investigate the legitimacy of the invasion of Grenada, remarked on his return, "There is no evidence that US nationals were being directly threatened."[50] And despite later evidence that some officials in Grenada considered "isolating" (not holding hostage) American citizens, no action then or at any other time before or during the invasion was taken against US citizens on Grenada.[51] Some congressmen thus appear merely to have caved in before the tide of the mass public's approval.

Other liberals felt cross-pressured by their commitments to international cooperation and human rights, observing that the OECS endorsed the intervention and that the Grenadian population and the democratic states of the Eastern Caribbean welcomed the invasion. And others still, learning what the RMC had done to its own comrades and fellow citizens on October 19, felt in retrospect that American citizens had to be rescued from a situation whose lack of proximate threat was overwhelmed by the extremity of the potential danger. A dearth of widely recognized US experts on the region and a delay in the announcement that the Governor General had reportedly invited the intervention compounded the liberals' confusion.[52] President Reagan thereby achieved the overwhelming endorsement of the American public despite the 1983 disaster in Lebanon. The United States lined up in support of the invasion—and against the world community, including some of this country's closest allies.

Farther from the Caribbean scene, the invasion met an equally overwhelming denunciation as a failure of multilateral security. In addition to usual political rivalries, the record of US intolerance for radical government in the third world made US claims to having attempted a rescue less than credible.

The Soviets, predictably, denounced the invasion as a "criminal act" of "international banditry" and, using the language of Nuremberg, a "crime against peace."[53] More important, like the invasion of Afghanistan and the Korean airliner incident, the invasion appears to have further disrupted whatever small prospects might have existed for a reduction in tensions along the central fronts of Soviet-American rivalry, such as arms control negotiations.

In Mexico City, thousands of young people rallied to denounce the invasion. The demonstration's organizer, drawing what he and many others saw as the wider implications of the invasion, announced, "This is a protest against the preparations the United States is making against Nicaragua and El Salvador."[54] The lopsided vote in the UN General Assembly (108 to 9) reflected additional sources of outrage at the United States' failure to consult either the United Nations or the OAS and at its "flagrant" violation of the UN Charter. Kirkpatrick took this occasion to call the United Nations "an outdated institution."[55]

For the Europeans, the invasion came as a particularly disturbing event. US allies, who were relying upon promises of close consultation as they began to deploy the Euromissile defense of the North Atlantic Treaty Organization, found all their fears of President Reagan's penchant for "cowboy" diplomacy reawakened. For British Prime Minister Margaret Thatcher, President Reagan's closest European ally, these concerns were magnified severalfold. Her government became acutely embarrassed when the Foreign Secretary, on assurances from the United States, in turn assured Parliament that no invasion was in the works—this the day before the invasion of a member of the Commonwealth that formally acknowledged the Queen as its sovereign. Queen Elizabeth II, in a rare display of public anger that sent a tremor through the British establishment, canceled her regular Tuesday audience with Prime Minister Thatcher.

Condemned by the world community and supported only by the Grenadians rescued, their immediate neighbors, and the United States (which for reasons peculiar to a temporary swing in its own political mood found an authentic rescue to be an opportunity to promote a convenient invasion), Grenada was a politically expensive success for its organizers, especially the United States.

Lessons?

When we consider the wider reasons for the escalation beyond Grenada and the Eastern Caribbean of the conflict that began with the 1979 NJM "revolution" and culminated with the coup and invasion of October 1983, the dependence and vulnerability of the typical ministate stand out.

The cost of providing security nationally is beyond the resources of ministates.[56] This is partly because the scope of national security has broadened. As citizens have come to expect from their governments economic development, social services, and the opportunity to participate in politics, so they have also come to expect that the state will keep their lives and livelihoods, not just their national borders, secure.[57] Small states have particular difficulties in providing this more extensive security domestically. Their dependence on outside forces that they cannot control is high. Small states generally lack ecological diversification and hence are especially vulnerable to natural disasters. A single hurricane or crop disease can destroy an entire economy. Small states such as Grenada also depend upon external sources for economic well-being, due to their small domestic markets, and for political stability, due to their vulnerability to coups. Added to this extensive external dependence, both the limited overseas representation of their foreign ministries and the large costs relative to national income of providing for national security independently contribute to their high demand for an international security regime.

Moreover, because their demand for external security is also highly unstable, ministates need insurance against large, though perhaps improbable, threats. Unstable demand occurs because their dependence varies with the issue or threat and because the most serious sources of dependency are not embraced within a regime they can collectively control.[58] Their lines of political and cultural interdependence are Caribbean; their extensive economic dependence runs to European or North American markets. Their security is threatened by domestic forces, by Caribbean attack or subversion, and by extra-regional intervention or even by interference from transnational criminal groups, such as those reportedly behind the attempted coup by Patrick John in Dominica in 1981.

Those are the circumstances that lead ministate crises to escalate unpredictably but rapidly. Unlike states enjoying strategic depth, their small size and limited resources for defense also make them especially vulnerable to foreign attack.[59] Together, these weaknesses leave them needing external sources of security and asking whether an alliance with a superpower, or regional multilateral security (the OECS or the OAS), or global multilateral security (the United Nations), or some combination of all three is necessary.

Direct alliance with an international power (the United States in this case) is clearly unsatisfactory. The enormous difference in the scale of resources threatens the independence of the ministate. An informal guarantee from the superpower to the minipower can, conversely, threaten neglect as the interests of the smaller are simply forgotten.

Traditionally, small states have thus responded to their vulnerability by being among the most fervent supporters of multilateral organizations.[60] But multilateral security regimes that allow or internalize the management of instability—global or continental security organizations such as the United Nations or the OAS—do not meet fully the security needs of ministates. First, the scale of the organization leaves the small Caribbean state without much voice in the management of its security. Second, large regional or global organizations are subject to international conflicts, such as the US-Soviet cold war, that complicate rather than ameliorate the security problems of small states by requiring them to join in these political disputes (to choose sides) and by hamstringing the large organizations in an emergency.[61]

More important, however, than these two problems in the operation of multilateral security for the smallest states is the unwillingness of large states to support the international organizations that could establish an effective supply of multilateral security for small states in the first place. Large states, such as the United States, have weak and unstable demands for multilateral security. While small states are "interdependent" with (dependent upon and vulnerable to) the large states, large states are not interdependently vulnerable to the small. The interest of large states in multilateral security is small, or at most occasional—designed to legitimize their presence abroad or to manage foreign, not national, security needs. (The OECS served this purpose for the United States in the Grenada invasion.) Large states reject multilateral cooperation's potentially constraining consequences, should it become effective. They thus do not tend to support the regular availability of the multilateral organization and forces that the smallest states need but cannot independently fund.[62]

The current Eastern Caribbean quasi-regime—the Regional Security System—established in 1982 and revived after the crisis in Grenada, appears to be at least a partial solution to the security dilemmas of the ministates. It attempts to lower the demand for multilateral security by raising the supply of national security. Britain is providing $3.5 million for coastal defenses. The United States has helped train and will, presumably, continue to fund eighty-to-ninety-person supplementary security forces, or "special services units," for each of the islands. Grenada will have a 650-person police force when training is completed.[63] A well-trained force of this size can deter and defend against the coups and private criminal threats that have plagued the islands and have led to so much concern on the part of the region's governments. These governments have agreed to respond to emergencies beyond the capacity of the national security force with a mobile strike force, coordinated by Barbados.

The necessity that a large majority of the region's states agree before they can assemble the military preponderance needed for an effective intervention probably protects the independence of the members from the prospect of the development of a single regional tyrant (Barbados?). But the creation of military forces, where before mild constabularies policed the Eastern Caribbean, poses new threats of creeping, domestic military oligarchy.[64] These forces will absorb government budgets needed for economic development. They also may pose threats to political stability, as Vaughan Lewis noted as early as 1982: "The fact of the matter is, however, that in small countries, the reinforcement of the local security systems leads to an upsetting of the balance between various socio-political sectors in the countries, giving the military, or national security sector, a decisive weight and a tendency to eventual preeminence in the political systems."[65]

Indeed, some Caribbean nationals and their governments are concerned that the new powers of collective regional security that are designed to protect their currently democratic states may make it difficult or impossible for domestic popular action to remove repressive regimes that may arise in the future, built around the security forces but still retaining "democratic" facades as did Gairy's Grenada. Given the great costs of disrupting ties between the islands of the Eastern Caribbean, few are optimistic that its states would be willing to take measures against a "thuggish" government with a democratic facade before it became a full tyranny. At the same time, Caribbean nationals fear that the regional force—without powerful extra-regional intervention—may not be effective against the new military oligarchies, whose power would be enhanced by the very military forces the Regional Security System established.

Ideally, should an extra-regional supplement to the local force be required, a multilateral organization such as the OAS or the United Nations would provide it. Ideally, as well, the multilateral organization could serve as a court of appeal, reducing the danger of a regional tyranny of the majority. But the multilateral supply of security is flawed in the ways discussed above, making Caribbean states dependent on US force and hence on US policy.

Notes

1. I am grateful for the advice I received on an earlier draft of this essay from Steven David and Ann Florini.

2. Inis Claude, *Swords Into Plowshares* (New York: Random House, 1971), Chapter 12.

3. See Robert Keohane, "The Demand for International Regimes," pp. 325–355, and Robert Jervis, "Security Regimes," pp. 375–378, both in *International Organization* 36 (2), for a discussion of the demand for and supply of international regimes. These issues are evaluated in the conclusion to this chapter.

4. British House of Commons second report of the Foreign Affairs Committee, *Grenada* (March 15, 1984), paras. 16–17. The other impressively thorough account on which I rely in this paper is Hugh O'Shaughnessy, *Grenada: Revolution, Invasion, and Aftermath* (London: Sphere Books, 1984).

5. US Departments of State and Defense, *Grenada: A Preliminary Report* (December 16, 1983).

6. *The New York Times*, December 5, 1984, charges that foreign sources of funding tied to the United States Republican party aided his electoral campaign.

7. Two very good introductions to the history of Grenada can be found in Archie W. Singham, *The Hero and the Crowd* (New Haven: Yale, 1968), Chapter 1, and in Gordon K. Lewis, *The Growth of the Modern West Indies* (New York: Monthly Review Press, 1968).

8. These figures come from the official Grenada Handbook of 1946, cited by W. Richard Jacobs and Ian Jacobs, *Grenada: Route to Revolution* (Havana: Casa de las Americas, 1980), p. 43. For extensive treatments of the effects of the plantation system in the Anglophonic Caribbean, see Franklin W. Knight, *The Caribbean* (New York: Oxford, 1978) and Sidney Mintz, *Caribbean Transformations* (Chicago: Aldine, 1974).

9. See Singham, op. cit. for the development of this interpretation.

10. O'Shaughnessy, op. cit. p. 69.

11. The nutmeg/mace trees were severely damaged in Hurricane Janet in 1955. Recovery in these crops has been steady, but competition from Indonesia has put pressure on prices. Tourist arrivals peaked in 1972–73, and following the revolution, the US government discouraged American tourists from vacationing in Grenada. See World Bank, *Memorandum on Grenada* (1982), pp. 4 and 9 for production and tourist tables.

12. Timothy Ashby, "Grenada: Soviet Stepping Stone," *U.S. Naval Proceedings* (December 1983), p. 30. This article also contains charges of a stronger Cuban

role in the coup: the presence of a team from the Cuban DGI (their CIA) and the arrival of the *Matanzas*, a Cuban ship with supplies, which arrived in St. Georges three days after the coup, although normal shipping time from Havana is seven days. The trip to Cuba and the acquisition of arms in New Orleans were described to me by Selwyn Strachan, former Minister of National Mobilization of the People's Revolutionary Government of Grenada during an interview in January 1982.

13. In January 1982 I was told by a Grenadian government minister that the UN vote was a mistake and that their intention had been to abstain. Information on cooperation with the Cuban delegations can be found in the Grenada documents seized during the invasion.

14. See Edward Cody's article, "Grenada Unsettles Its Neighbors, But So Does U.S.," *The Washington Post*, April 24, 1983.

15. See the minutes of the meeting between national security adviser Clark, Deputy Secretary of State Dam, Prime Minister Bishop, and aides. Clark threatened the withdrawal of the American Medical School at St. Georges, a major source of funds, if Grenada did not abandon its link with Cuba and change its form of government.

16. Castro's denunciation of the murder of Bishop took place immediately and also as part of a long speech, a post-mortem, on the Grenadian revolution, "Declaration of the Party and Revolutionary Government of Cuba Regarding the Events in Grenada," Havana, October 20, 1983. And see Alan Berger's article, "Grenada According to Castro," *The Boston Globe*, November 20, 1983. Rumors of a planned Cuban counter-coup were reported by Democratic Senator Daniel P. Moynihan of New York and the Miami Cuban community. According to reports, Colonel Tortolo has since been stripped of his rank, reduced to private, and sent to Angola as a punishment for having failed to mount an effective defense of Grenada. *The Washington Post*, October 25, 1984.

17. I have reason to doubt that there was a written request (written *before* the intervention) for an outside intervention. But Governor General Sir Paul Scoon claims to have made a request for outside "help" before the intervention. And Prime Minister Adams of Barbados claims to have received the request through a Western ambassador to Grenada. See "Speech of Prime Minister J.M.G.M. Adams Before Parliament on November 15, 1983," Annex C of the House of Commons second report, *Grenada*, op. cit. Prime Minister George Chambers of Trinidad and Tobago, who did not support the OECS/US intervention, also claims to have received an expression of interest in outside help from Sir Paul conveyed to the President of Trinidad and Tobago (see Annex D of the same report). Sir Paul, however, did not directly make a request for outside help to the British High Commissioner when the High Commissioner visited him during the Governor General's house arrest on Sunday, October 22. This has led many sources (see *The Economist*, March 10, 1984) to doubt that there ever was a request; others argue that the danger the Governor General was in, together with Britain's lack of interest in the earlier request for assistance made by the OECS, made the Governor General unlikely to trust his safety to an official, possibly publicized, request made to the government of Britain.

18. Trinidad and Tobago and Guyana, both of which later opposed the invasion, had condemned the coup and the killings, and had voted for the Trinidad resolution at the CARICOM meeting. This resolution included a strong condemnation of the coup and the killings. Trinidad had unilaterally immediately embargoed Grenada. But many Caribbean diplomats questioned the sincerity of Guyana's position, some going so far as to suggest that it was Guyana, itself the target of an earlier CARICOM condemnation for corrupt and coercive electoral practices, that warned the RMC of the impending invasion.

19. See the speech before Parliament by Prime Minister Chambers of Trinidad and Tobago, Appendix D of the House of Commons second report, *Grenada*, op. cit.

20. See the text of the letter, dated October 23, 1983, from the OECS to the United States requesting US help in *The New York Times*, October 25, 1983.

21. The Caribbean region and CARICOM, however, have long suffered from meager economic integration, making CARICOM a common market that has little complementarity. Local economists complain of the "guava jam, guava jelly" syndrome, referring to the problem that economies concentrating on the production of goods such as the first or the second tend to have little basis for mutually advantageous trade.

22. Prime Minister Eugenia Charles, press conference with President Reagan at the White House, October 25, 1983, transcript in *The Wall Street Journal*, October 26, 1983.

23. Quoted in a speech, "The Larger Importance of Grenada," before the Associated Press Managing Editors Conference, Louisville, Kentucky, by Deputy Secretary of State Dam, November 4, 1983.

24. O'Shaughnessy, op. cit. pp. 133–139 for an account of the popular demonstration and the massacre. But the exact manner of Creft's death has not been confirmed; bodies were destroyed.

25. See George Quester, "Trouble in the Islands: Defending the Microstates," *International Security*, Vol. 8, No. 2, pp. 160–175, a general account of the problem of microstate security. Ambassador John Connell of the Barbados Mission to the UN in the interview cited above offered a number of accounts of the activities of dissident groups and of the vulnerability of the islands to politically and criminally inspired attacks.

26. Deputy Secretary Dam, "The Larger Importance of Grenada."

27. US consular officers were advised that their aircraft landing at Greenville was fired upon by soldiers on the ground. They were placed under constant military escort. They observed widespread patrols of soldiers and a public atmosphere of apprehension following the murders and the shoot-on-sight curfew. After they reported their apprehensions to Ambassador Bish in Barbados, the Ambassador recommended an immediate evacuation to avoid another Iranian-style hostage crisis. Source: interview at the US State Department with Ambassador Charles Gillespie, September 14, 1984.

28. An account of the US decision process can be found in Assistant Secretary of State Langhorne Motley's statement before the House Armed Services Committee (January 24, 1984), Annex E of the House of Commons second report, *Grenada*, op. cit.

29. As reported in "Britain's Grenada Shut-out," *The Economist*, March 10, 1984, p. 32.

30. *The New York Times*, October 28, 1983.

31. President Reagan, "Peace and National Security," televised address to the nation, Washington, DC, March 23, 1983, p. 40 in the US State Department's *Realism, Strength, Negotiation* (May 1984). These specific interests gained an increased significance from the Reagan administration's Grand Strategy—the need to wage a new cold war to protect an America perceived to be under an extreme global strategic threat and locked in an ideological contest with the Soviet Union. For an influential statement of this view, see Richard M. Nixon, *The Real War* (New York: Warner, 1980), especially Chapter 1.

32. Secretary Shultz, "Democratic Solidarity in the Americas," luncheon remarks to leaders of Barbados, Jamaica, and OECS members, Bridgetown, February 6, 1984, p. 133 in US State Department op. cit. *The Economist*, March 10, 1984, p. 32 reported a Reagan adviser's comments on the invasion along these same lines: "The purpose was to deny the Russians/Cubans a feeling of potency in grabbing small vulnerable states in the region. It had to be nipped in the bud before it developed into another Cuba."

33. President Reagan, "America's Foreign Policy Challenges for the 1980s," address before the Center for Strategic and International Studies, Washington, DC, April 6, 1984, p. 11 in US State Department, op. cit.

34. Cole Blasier, *The Hovering Giant* (Pittsburgh: University of Pittsburgh Press, 1976) is a survey of US policy toward the wider region. The geo-economic and sea-lanes view can be found in Timothy Ashby, "Grenada: Threat to America's Oil Routes," *National Defense* (May-June, 1981), pp. 52–54, 205. David Ronfeldt, *Geopolitics, Security, and U.S. Strategy in the Caribbean Basin* (R.2997-AF/RC) (Santa Monica: Rand, 1983) provides a sophisticated argument for the strategic value of US hegemony (which he calls "collective hegemony") over the Caribbean. For an alternative view, see the testimony by Jorge Dominguez and Richard Feinberg in *Hearings on The Caribbean Basin Policy*, House of Representatives, Committee on Foreign Affairs, Subcommittee on Inter-American Affairs, 97th Cong. 1st sess., July 14–28, 1981; and see Michael Doyle, "Squaring the Circle of Crisis: President Reagan's Cold War in the Caribbean," paper presented at the Conference on Geopolitical Change in the Caribbean, C.E.E.S.T.E.M., San Jeronimo Lidice, Mexico, April 1982.

35. Michael Massing, "Grenada Before and After," *The Atlantic Monthly* (February 1984), p. 81. And see Anthony P. Maingot, "American Foreign Policy in the Caribbean," *International Journal* XI (Spring 1985).

36. See Massing, op. cit. p. 83, citing *The Washington Post*, February 27, 1983.

37. See the minutes of the meeting between the three and a Grenadian aide in the Grenada documents.

38. The quotation is in the House of Commons second report, *Grenada*, Appendix E, op. cit.

39. Although the operation was an operation of the OECS, it was not an operation by the OECS. It was planned and conducted by an ad hoc group of

states, including most of the OECS, Jamaica, Barbados, and, most obviously from a military standpoint, the United States. In this respect, the Grenada operation resembled the multinational force sent to Beirut. For the legal debate (including a discussion on whether the operation conformed to the letter of the OECS Charter), see the articles by C. Joyner, John Norton Moore, and Detlev Vagts in the *American Journal of International Law*, Vol. 78, No. 1 (January 1984).

40. *The New York Times*, November 6, 1983.

41. Poll by St. Augustine Research Associates of Trinidad and Tobago reported in *The Nation* (Barbados), January 20, 1984.

42. Charles's comment in transcript of press conference, *The Wall Street Journal*, October 26, 1983.

43. O'Shaughnessy suggests that the OECS should have waited and blockaded the island if the RMC failed to accept the terms of the Trinidad-CARICOM resolution. He notes the extreme vulnerability of Grenada to blockade, since all of the island's energy supplies were imported (p. 220). But to the leaders of the OECS, a blockade was less acceptable than an invasion. It would have forced the people of Grenada and their relatives into the front lines and used the suffering of Grenadian citizens to pressure a government that had already revealed on October 19 the quality of its concern for its citizens.

44. Interviews with Ambassador John Connell (Barbados Mission to the UN), Charles Fleming (St. Lucia Mission to the UN), and a US official. Concerning OAS attitudes toward the Anglophonic Caribbean, Caribbean officials cite experiences similar to Grenada's: in 1974, Grenada was accepted for membership in the World Bank and the Caribbean Development Bank, and was turned down by the Inter-American Development Bank (see O'Shaughnessy, op. cit. p. 69).

45. *The New York Times*, October 26, 1983.

46. *The New York Times*, November 4, 1983.

47. An ABC/Washington Post poll reported in *Time*, November 21, 1983, p. 17. The approval rating specifically for the Grenada invasion rose to 65 percent of the American public, 27 percent disapproving, according to James Dickerson's article, "Bombing, Invasion in Eerie Focus," *The Washington Post*, October 24, 1984.

48. Michael Mandelbaum and William Schneider, "The New Internationalism," pp. 34–88 of K. Oye, D. Rothschild, and R. Lieber, eds., *Eagle Entangled* (New York: Longman, 1979).

49. William Schneider, "Conservatism, Not Interventionism: Trends in Foreign Policy Opinion, 1974–1983," pp. 33–64 of K. Oye, R. Lieber, and D. Rothschild, eds., *Eagle Defiant* (Boston: Little Brown, 1983).

50. Quoted by Hedrick Smith in his article, "Members of House Differ on Invasion," *The New York Times*, November 10, 1983.

51. Reported in a study by Dr. Michael Ledeen commissioned by the US State and Defense Departments. *The Washington Post*, October 5, 1984.

52. Congressman O'Neill at first denounced the invasion as gunboat diplomacy and then a week later deemed it justified. *Time* magazine at first treated the invasion as another Afghanistan, then in the following week's issue as a legitimate rescue.

53. See Dusko Doder's article, "Moscow Assails Reagan for Grenada Invasion," *The Washington Post*, October 26, 1983.

54. *The New York Times*, November 10, 1983.

55. Quoted in O'Shaughnessy, op. cit. p. 186. According to sources at the US Mission to the United Nations, neither the Mission nor Kirkpatrick was informed of the invasion before its occurrence, reflecting Washington's lack of interest, it seems, in any UN role in the dispute.

56. Keohane, op. cit. p. 338. I have rephrased the lack of a clear scheme of liability as uncertain but extensive interdependence.

57. Richard H. Ullman, "Redefining Security," *International Security*, Vol. 8, No. 1, pp. 129–153 discusses the wider aspects of contemporary international security. For some small states, the rights described in the UN's Universal Declaration of Human Rights can be protected only internationally.

58. Jervis notes that the supply of security will also depend on technical factors such as whether offensive weapons are distinguishable from defensive and whether one or the other is dominant. Defense dominance and distinguishability favor international cooperation. In the special strategic situation of ministates, however, it is generally difficult to distinguish offensive from defensive weapons. (Add fishing boats to a large defensive force and it becomes a large offensive force; and Bishop's coup was staged by forty-six lightly armed and little-trained followers.) Neither one nor the other is conquest-dominant in defense or offense, but the offense's capacity to disrupt far surpasses the defense's capacity to protect. The offense can attack a small island, and whether it conquers or not, escape without significant consequences. "Cooperation Under the Security Dilemma," *World Politics* 30 (1) (1978), p. 362.

59. An extensive review of the literature on small states can be found in Amstrup Niels, "The Perennial Problem of Small States: A Survey of Research Efforts," *Cooperation and Conflict*, Vol. II, No. 3 (1976), pp. 163–182.

60. Claude, op. cit. Chapter 12 is a good survey of these issues. And see Sean Lester, "The Far East Dispute from the Point of View of the Small States," in *Problems of Peace*, Eighth Series (London: Allen and Unwin, 1933), reprinted in Joel Larus, ed., *From Collective Security to Preventive Diplomacy* (New York: Wiley, 1965), pp. 118–125. The League and the UN became focuses of their diplomacy.

61. Ernst Haas, "Regime Decay: Conflict Management and International Organization: 1945–1981," *International Organization* 37, No. 2 (Spring, 1983). Haas describes the need for very wide consensus for the effective operation of multilateral security, p. 207. He shows the harmful effects of the cold war on multilateral security on p. 206.

62. See Kenneth Waltz, *Theory of International Politics* (Reading, Massachusetts: Addison-Wesley, 1979), Chapter Seven, for a discussion of these issues that is telling for security interdependence.

63. "U.S. Post-Invasion Image Rests on New Airport," *The Washington Post*, October 25, 1984. And see David Simmons, "Militarization of the Caribbean," *International Journal* XI (Spring 1985).

64. The attempted Patrick John coup in Dominica in 1981, as one example, involved former members of the island's security force who had been fired in a budget retrenchment. There have also been coup attempts in St. Vincent (1979).

65. Vaughan Lewis, "The U.S. and the Caribbean," *Caribbean Review* No. 2 (1982), p. 51.

Conclusions: A Mix of Means

Arthur R. Day

The foregoing chapters have examined two closely related aspects of international security: first, the potential for local conflicts to escalate to the point at which they bring dangerous confrontations between the superpowers; and second, the means available to the international community to contain or to resolve local conflicts. On the basis of so few case studies there can be no pretense of universal validity for the results of our examination. The conflicts studied are important ones, however, that represent a variety of characteristic types, and they can be helpful in suggesting conclusions on both issues.

The Danger of Escalation

Many believe that the most likely trigger for World War III, should it ever occur, will be a local conflict that has escalated beyond its own region and ultimately draws in the superpowers. This belief flows readily from the premise on which the collective-security concept is based, namely that the international security system is an interrelated whole, all parts of which are affected by a breakdown in any one part. Collective security is paid lip service today, but governments reveal by their behavior that they do not believe that the security of all is affected by a threat to the security of any one of them. Their skepticism is understandable, given the 200 or more conflicts that have been identified as having occurred since 1945 without having led to a war that pitted major powers against each other, let alone the superpowers. What do our six cases suggest about escalation?

None of the conflicts examined showed a significant tendency to escalate beyond the region. Peacekeeping forces from outside the region intervened in Chad and in Lebanon, but only in Chad did extra-regional troops have more than a peacekeeping role, when the French moved in to counter the Libyan invasion in 1983. Even in this latter role, France was never close to hostilities with Libya on a state-to-state level. This was a case of outside forces being drawn into an arena of conflict without that conflict's spreading beyond the confines of the arena itself.

The war between Ethiopia and Somalia was one in which the superpowers backed opposing sides—changing sides in doing so, a situation that might have suggested the danger of escalation. In fact, however, Harbeson finds that the superpowers behaved more moderately toward each other in relation to this conflict than was the case at that time in their direct bilateral relationship. In addition, actions by regional states to contain, to disaggregate, and to define the conflict drained away some of the pressures that might have led to escalation.

The Lebanese civil war seemed also at times to contain the danger of superpower conflict, not from peacekeeping interventions or from the domestic struggle itself but from the interventions of Syria and Israel, client states respectively of the Soviet Union and the United States. Until 1981 these two regional powers took some pains to avoid direct confrontation, but in that year they clashed in the air over Lebanon. A year later, in the course of the massive Israeli invasion of Lebanon, serious ground fighting occurred between them. Both sides refrained, however, from escalating their encounters to full-scale state-to-state warfare. As in the case of Chad, these outside forces were drawn into the arena without the conflict's spilling over into their own territories. The superpowers, despite an unwise claim by the United States that its military presence in Lebanon in 1982–83 was a barrier to Soviet expansion, have never come close to significant confrontation over Lebanon.

The Iran-Iraq war has taken place in a neuralgic corner of the world, in the heart of the oil-producing region vital to the West and close to Soviet borders. Nevertheless, the superpowers have refrained from becoming involved sufficiently that tension has not arisen between them as a result of the war. It is interesting that one of the parties to the conflict, Iraq, attempted to heighten international concern and to attract political intervention by itself escalating the stakes in the so-called tanker war, but had little success.

The policies pursued by Washington and Moscow in the invasions of Afghanistan and Grenada, respectively, have also been effective in avoiding serious confrontation, although tension certainly has resulted in both cases. These were situations that escalated quickly from local, largely internal, dimensions to the superpower level, but held at that point with only one superpower significantly and overtly involved. The United States provides covert assistance to the struggle against the Soviet Union in Afghanistan, and Moscow supported the Revolutionary Military Council after the bloody coup in Grenada. Yet each power has tacitly acknowledged that the military operation of the other—the Soviet Union in Afghanistan and the United States in Grenada—took place in the other's sphere of influence and made no move to intervene militarily against it.

While superpower conflict has not been a danger in any of the disputes, escalation[1] was of special interest in at least three of them: Lebanon, Chad, and Iran-Iraq. The escalations were of different types, however, and it is useful to distinguish three broad categories, especially as they occurred in the latter two conflicts. The first is escalation of the original dispute, as the fighting in Lebanon, for example, expanded from a shooting incident to a conflict involving thousands of fighters in a dozen or more militias. The second, of more interest to this study, is the introduction of increased force by an outside agency—in these cases, governments—for the purpose of gaining some control or influence over the conflict, such as through the creation of a stalemate. French interventions in Chad and the 1976 Syrian intervention in Lebanon were of this type. The third is the introduction of force by an outside government for unilateral national advantage, not necessarily directly related to the basic dispute. Libya's 1983 invasion of Chad, to annex territory, and Israel's invasions of Lebanon in 1978 and 1982, to attack the Palestine Liberation Organization (PLO), were the clearest examples. Zartman in his article on Chad looks at interventions designed to control or influence a conflict and distinguishes between two types: escalations to raise— to break a stalemate—and escalations to call—to create a stalemate.

To the extent that the six conflicts examined in this volume are representative, it would appear that local conflicts in the third world are not at all likely to touch off war between the superpowers. Intervention by a superpower in the third world, so long as it occurs in the sphere of influence of the superpower involved, seems also unlikely to produce such a confrontation. The superpowers would appear, however, to be very sensitive to crisis occurring in their own respective spheres of influence. Why this is so would be the subject of another study focused on the strategic relationship of the superpowers. The four examples in this volume of conflicts between third world opponents, civil or international, suggest that in today's global security environment the gap between such local wars and the superpower nuclear balance is so great that a spark would leap across it only in the most unique circumstances. The toleration of violence that is such a marked characteristic of international life today stems in part, certainly, from a widespread assumption that the nuclear fuse is in fact relatively well-insulated from regional conflict.

A first conclusion suggested by this apparent stability of the global security system is that the international community need not feel compelled to manage or to resolve every local conflict that arises. But conflicts have costs other than the danger of larger war: human suffering, physical destruction, the setback of economic progress, the creation of enduring enmities and tensions, and the degrading of international life generally. It is obviously desirable to prevent or to ameliorate such costs even though the urgency of doing so may not be of the same magnitude as the urgency of preventing escalation to major war. Conflicts can be approached deliberately when they seem ripe for fruitful intervention. When the interests of other states in or outside the region are immediately and seriously affected, prompt and intensive efforts at managing or resolving the dispute would presumably be called for. The discussion that follows will assume that, for one reason or another, states outside the conflict have decided that intervention is necessary, and it will focus primarily on the question of the most effective means.

A wide variety of methods has been used in attempts to manage or to resolve regional conflicts. They have been undertaken by individual states, by ad hoc groups of states, by regional or other sub-global international organizations, and by the United Nations. It is of interest to know how effective these different forms of intervention have been— whether multilateral or national efforts have been more effective, for example—as well as to distinguish the types of results each seems to have been best-suited to achieve—arranging cease-fires, mediating disputes, mounting peacekeeping operations, and so forth.

Multilateral Means—the United Nations

The United Nations has been engaged in all six of the disputes studied, although its involvement with the Chadian civil war was essentially to hand it back to the Organization of African Unity (OAU). With respect to the other five, the world body played one or more of a wide variety of roles that could be categorized roughly as follows:

- judgments and decisions of the two political deliberative bodies— the General Assembly and the Security Council;
- actions by the Secretary General and his subordinates, ranging from statements of exhortation, warning, etc. to elaborate efforts of good offices and mediation;
- the functional but in practice highly political role of providing peacekeeping forces, organized and managed by the Secretariat under Security Council mandates; and
- purely functional roles by UN agencies ameliorating the conditions or consequences of the conflicts, such as care for refugees.

The General Assembly and the Security Council

The actions by the General Assembly and the Security Council were essentially actions by member states. They did not end or materially modify the conflicts and were not expected to, except in the case of the Council resolution calling on Israel to withdraw its forces from Lebanon after its March 1978 invasion. Here, however, it was primarily US pressure on Israel that brought this result, while the operative UN role was the provision of a peacekeeping force. The resolutions adopted by the Assembly and the Council in the other cases were not entirely without effect—the resounding majorities in the Assembly against the Soviet invasion of Afghanistan and against the invasion of Grenada by the United States and the Organization of Eastern Caribbean States (OECS) both went beyond the routine political jousting that characterizes so much of the activity in the Assembly and the Council. To this extent they represented clear reflections of standards held by the international community. In the case of Afghanistan, useful principles to govern a settlement were established.

Because of the partisan political character of so many Council and Assembly actions, Israel has come to regard the United Nations as politically hostile and deeply prejudiced against it. It regarded as merely reflecting this bias the Council resolutions calling on it to cease its 1978 and 1982 invasions of Lebanon. The wielding of the United Nations, so to speak, by powerful member state factions to promote their own partisan purposes undermines the organization's capacity to play an effective role in conflict management. The Council resolution on the Iran-Iraq war, in failing to place blame where it clearly belonged, on Iraq, was patently prejudiced and had little effect except to reduce even further Iran's willingness to cooperate with the United Nations.

The cases that did not come before either UN body are also instructive in defining the character that UN deliberations, decisions, and actions have come to have and the way that they are perceived and used by member states. Taking a dispute to the United Nations is frequently seen as "internationalizing" it. Parties to the Lebanese civil conflict from time to time considered whether this was tactically desirable. The side that felt itself to have the upper hand locally in military terms was naturally disinclined to internationalize it, whereas the weaker side tended to look outside the conflict for support. The Moslem left moved from strength to weakness in early 1976 and shifted simultaneously from opposing the internationalization of the problem to urging it. That the dispute was domestic and hence not appropriate for UN consideration was an argument to be advanced or ignored depending on one's tactical position, although there seemed to be an underlying sentiment in Lebanon and in the United Nations that the issues of local power-sharing could not be dealt with usefully at the international level. Syria was, throughout, primarily interested in control and generally considered that opening the issue to debate by the international community, including Syria's opponents, was not compatible with this goal. Why Damascus decided on one occasion to depart from this policy—in the Arab League summit of October 1976—was instructive and will be considered later.

Harbeson argues that neither Ethiopia nor Somalia, for separate reasons, considered it advantageous to take their conflict to the United Nations, which had earlier attempted to arbitrate the border problem but had failed because of disagreement over the terms of reference. Ethiopia did not recognize the existence of an international issue, while Somalia asserted that the issue existed but realized that its position would not be supported in the United Nations.

Doyle found that the states planning the Grenada invasion did not consider taking the crisis to the United Nations (at least representatives attending the planning meetings could recall no such consideration). The United Nations, in the perception of Eastern Caribbean leaders, was incapable of rapid or effective action. The US government, especially under the Reagan administration, would have had the same view of the United Nations, but even more importantly would have been unwilling to involve in this neighborhood conflict the Soviet Union and the many leftist-oriented governments of the third world that would have had a voice in any UN deliberations on the issue.

The Secretary General and the Secretariat

The most effective UN interventions were those of the Secretary General and his subordinates in the UN Secretariat, including the setting up of peacekeeping operations. (Although it is a hybrid—including a Security Council mandate and Secretariat implementation—peacekeeping has been relatively so successful because of its implementation by the Secretariat.) This is not to say that the Secretary General and his subordinates met with a high degree of success. They did not. But they grappled in a serious and purposeful way with specific issues, both large and limited, obtained the more or less respectful attention of the parties, and achieved some positive results.

The Secretary General has been more active in the Iran-Iraq conflict than in any of the other five cases. Within months after the start of the war in 1980, he sent Olof Palme—who had been and subsequently again became Swedish Prime Minister—to work out a halt to the fighting and an invitation to negotiations. This ambitious effort failed, and UN officials turned to more narrowly targeted efforts to limit the consequences of the fighting: efforts to free ships trapped by the war in the Shatt al-Arab waterway, efforts to establish a moratorium on attacks against civilians, and efforts to end the use of chemical weapons and to improve the treatment of prisoners of war. One effort failed; others were partially or at least temporarily successful. A clear achievement was the stationing of UN observers in both countries to check for attacks on civilians.

Eventually the search for a broader winding down of the conflict was resumed, looking toward what UN officials described as "de facto peace." This imaginative concept had the aim of pruning away by mutual agreement the actual manifestations of conflict without at first trying to resolve the basic dispute. Ultimately, it was hoped, success would create an atmosphere conducive to peace negotiations. These efforts have so far failed but continue to offer a way to deal with a conflict that is stalemated but that one side or the other (in this case, Iran) refuses to abandon.

It is interesting and instructive that the Secretary General and his subordinates have been able to win the confidence of both sides sufficiently to pursue these efforts. Iran regards the United Nations, as an organization of member states, to be strongly biased against it, primarily because of the Security Council's failure to condemn Iraq for starting the war—a failure that did indeed reveal a bias among UN member states against Iran. Secretariat officials have been able to distance themselves from the membership and the deliberative bodies—the General Assembly and the Security Council—and to establish their own separate reputation for fairness and balance with both sides. Without that, they could not have been useful.

The Secretary General has also undertaken a good-offices role in the Afghan conflict. A senior UN official was appointed to establish contact with the Afghan and Pakistani governments, Pakistan in effect representing the interests of the Afghan population and the Afghan government speaking for the Soviets. Beginning in 1982, a series of conferences—proximity talks—has been held in Geneva under UN sponsorship, with the Secretary General's representative acting as go-between for the participants, who have refused to meet directly. There has been little or no progress toward a settlement and the war continues unabated, but as Dupree points out, the Geneva conference framework and the activity of the UN representative provide an already agreed-upon diplomatic forum in which to work out a solution when and if the military/political situation dictates. In addition, there is substantial agreement on three instruments already negotiated. Completion is held up by slow progress on a fourth instrument that will cover the issue of troop withdrawal and would relate all four instruments to one another.

The Lebanese war differs from the other cases being studied in that it consists of several conflicts superimposed on one another. The United Nations has had little or no part to play in dealing with the issues of the basic, domestic dispute. But the Secretariat has engaged in various good-offices activities, as well as in a major peacekeeping operation, in trying to limit hostilities, primarily where non-Lebanese have been involved. A middle-grade member of the Secretariat in New York has spent a large proportion of his time in Lebanon for this purpose, and a senior official has frequently gone out, as well. The United Nations had military observers in the country at the outbreak of the war, stemming from the armistice agreement of 1949 and the establishment of the United Nations Truce Supervisory Organization (UNTSO) to monitor it. The observers operated on the Lebanese side of the Israeli-Lebanese border, with a headquarters in Beirut. They manned a vehicle crossing point at Ras Naqoura, where the border reaches the Mediterranean Sea. The observers have remained in Lebanon during the prolonged conflict. They have provided resources on the scene to help in the UN's discreet and largely backstage activities, and the crossing point has become an important entryway.

The single most important UN intervention in Lebanon was the setting up of the United Nations Interim Force in Lebanon (UNIFIL) in the spring of 1978. UNIFIL was intended primarily as a peacekeeping force for the southern Lebanese border area, but there was no peace to be kept. Such a situation presents special difficulties for a peacekeeping force, even one that has the approval of the UN member states concerned. The forces among which order was to be maintained in Lebanon were sub-national, neither represented in the United Nations themselves nor under the firm control of any government that was so represented. In such a situation, reliable commitments to cooperate with the peacekeeping unit cannot be obtained by the United Nations from the forces that count, at least under current procedures. A government that is unsympathetic to the operation, as Israel was in this case, can undercut it through irregular forces over which it has control but for which it has no formal responsibility. The job of maintaining order is therefore less one of monitoring a peace already arranged between two parties—the classic peacekeeping formula—than it is a constabulary function of establishing and maintaining order by use of force. This a UN peacekeeping force is not mandated to do. It is not usually large enough nor heavily enough armed to do so, and in any case the member states providing the individual units that compose it would not likely agree to such an active combat role.

What is perhaps most instructive about UNIFIL, though, is that it was put into Lebanon not primarily to keep the peace but to help induce the Israelis to withdraw their forces. Not that Israel believed the UN unit would make the continued presence of its own troops unnecessary; it had no confidence in the United Nations. Rather, the Security Council's decision to insert UNIFIL made it more difficult for Israel to insist on retaining some of its national forces in Lebanon, and thus the Council's action gave the United States the extra leverage it needed to press the Israelis to withdraw. In one sense, this was a misuse of UN peacekeeping, since the circumstances were not fully appropriate for it (as its vague and overly ambitious mandate showed). In another sense, the United Nations did play an important part in forestalling what many feared would be a larger Middle East war if Israeli forces remained in close proximity to Syrian troops stationed in Lebanon. The presence of UNIFIL also made continuously available on the spot a senior UN officer for assisting in other efforts to control the conflict, an example being the force commander's role in negotiating a cease-fire, jointly with a US diplomat, between Israel and the PLO in 1981. This officer is under the direction of the Secretary General and the Secretariat and can be used by them, within discreet limits, as their representative in a conflict-management role extending beyond peacekeeping per se.

It is evident that the United Nations has been much more significantly involved in Lebanon, despite its being at heart a domestic conflict, than in any other of the six cases. Why is this so? One answer is that the Lebanese conflict became, in part at least, a dimension of the larger Arab-Israeli struggle. The question thus becomes: why is the United Nations so deeply involved in the Arab-Israeli struggle? Historically, of course, the modern form of the conflict was born in the United Nations, with the partition resolution of 1947. UN institutions for the care of Palestinian refugees and the monitoring of armistice lines have been in the Middle East since the earliest days. That the struggle continues to attract intense UN involvement, however, is mainly a result of two factors: the interest and concern that the conflict continues to excite among important powers, especially superpowers; and the fact that, for much of the third world, it lies along the old colonial fault-line, with Israel cast as the colonial power.

The intervention of the Secretariat in the Grenada operations was much less major but was of some significance, nonetheless. A fact-finding mission headed by a senior Secretariat official was sent to Grenada after the fighting had ended. It was dispatched by the General Assembly and reported back to that body. By this means the UN professional staff was able to convey to the member states a credible, first-hand, balanced account of the state of affairs, which in this case gave little basis for further criticism of the United States and the other states involved in the invasion.

UN Functional Activities

The final category of UN intervention—purely functional activities—can be thought of on two levels. The most obvious and most immediate in its application to specific conflicts is the care of refugees, the provision of emergency supplies to stricken populations, and the like. The other level is more basic—long-term economic development, education programs, the coordination of international activity such as transport and communications that could cause disputes if left undealt with, the elimination of human rights abuses, and other activities that can help eradicate or reduce sources of tension and conflict. The latter category would require a separate study in itself and cannot be examined here. But it is worth noting that many UN functions that seem social, economic, or humanitarian also can have a significant, long-term political-security dimension.

So far as our six cases are concerned, the United Nations has had functional roles of the more immediate sort in two of them: Lebanon and the Ethiopia-Somalia conflict. In Lebanon, the primary UN functional responsibility has been the care of Palestinian refugees who fled the areas that became part of Israel in 1948. While the need for this refugee support has not arisen out of the civil war in Lebanon, the presence of the UN infrastructure and personnel has given the organization a continuing link to the conflict in which the refugees and their camps have been much involved. In Ethiopia and Somalia, the United Nations has cared for the refugees from the conflict between the two states and has negotiated the repatriation of some of them.

Regional and Other Nonuniversal Organizations

Regional or other organizations of a nonuniversal character have been involved in all six conflicts. In one of them, the invasion of Grenada, a sub-regional organization helped organize and then fully endorsed a military intervention. In the two African cases—Ethiopia-Somalia and Chad—the regional organization exercised some influence by reaffirming principles of importance in the conflicts but otherwise was not able to manage or to resolve them. The Arab League intervened to some effect at an early stage of the Lebanese conflict but had little influence on the longer-run development of the war. A variety of organizations has taken an interest in the Iran-Iraq war and in the Soviet invasion of Afghanistan, coordinating the reaction of member states or offering to play a good-offices or mediatory role.

The Grenada case is the only one of the six in which a multilateral organization acted decisively and effectively to deal with a security problem. The threat to regional security was the domestic coup against Grenadian Prime Minister Maurice Bishop and the substitution of a more militant government. This threat was removed by the intervention of the Organization of Eastern Caribbean States, joined by the United States. Looked at from the perspective of this study, however, the question arises as to whether the action can be regarded as an example of multilateral intervention or must be considered basically unilateral. The best answer seems to be that it was a hybrid. It was not a unilateral action cloaked post facto with a flimsy multilateral gesture—as was the case with Syrian intervention in Lebanon, for example. The need was genuinely felt in the region; the Caribbean states lacked the necessary military muscle; and a multilateral process was set in motion by the OECS countries separate from US involvement. To that degree it was a regional multilateral endeavor.

What made the operation such a dubious model for providing security to small states was the overwhelming character of the superpower involvement. Although the intervention was a hybrid, the utterly dominant power of the United States, so out of scale with the size and strength of other states involved, gave it the character of a unilateral action—a superpower acting as regional policeman. In this case the superpower action produced a result almost universally welcomed in the countries most immediately concerned. The problem, as Doyle describes it, is, of course, that the strength that produced this desirable result was not in any reliable sense under the control of the countries most affected by it. The United States had its own agenda that only partly overlapped with theirs. They could feel no assurance whatever that the same strength would always be deployed for purposes they saw as compatible with their interests. To put it another way, if a sub-regional grouping such as the OECS could be certain that the muscle of the superpower would be employed only when the grouping decided that it should be, the model would be a reassuring one of true multilateral security. But to state the proposition is to recognize how far it is from reality.

In the two African cases—the Ethiopian-Somalian war and the Chadian civil dispute—the Organization of African Unity recognized a responsibility for moderating and resolving the conflicts. As Harbeson and Zartman make clear, however, it was largely ineffective in dealing with them. It did excercise an influence on the development and outcome of the two conflicts, though, by reaffirming principles of central importance to them. In the Ethiopian-Somalian case, this principle was the unacceptability of border modifications that favored Ethiopia. In Chad, it was the principle of state legitimacy, which favored the sitting government of Hissen Habré.

In the Chadian case, the OAU was more enterprising than in the Horn of Africa, but still unimpressive in its performance. In the end, despite much deliberation and some decisions, including the dispatch of a peacekeeping force, it failed to have a real impact on the conflict. The fault in peacekeeping seemed to be a profound lack of clarity among member state governments about their purposes and goals, coupled with inefficiency at every level in carrying out what decisions were eventually made. The peacekeeping force met with somewhat the same problems as UNIFIL had met with in Lebanon: a chaotic local situation and an unclear mandate impossible to carry out in the circumstances. In the case of the OAU force, however, it simply withdrew after a brief and ineffective period. Zartman's conclusion is that there is no remedy for the failure of the OAU and of individual states and ad hoc groups of states but that African leaders must come to an awareness of their responsibilities. Such a verdict does not offer much hope for an early change in this pattern of failure.

The other intervention by a regional organization in a case under study was the cease-fire and peacekeeping operation established by the Arab League in Lebanon in October 1976. The cease-fire worked in part because, having been imposed multilaterally, it was supported by the governments that had been fanning the flames of civil conflict through their backing of rival Lebanese factions. Zartman speaks of diplomatic measures being necessary in Chad to seal off external support to the rebellion. The same principle was involved in the Lebanese cease-fire, and it illustrated two lessons about multilateral security: first, governments are not likely to put aside their own rival interests for the purpose of halting a conflict unless they become more concerned about the consequences of the conflict than about those rival interests; and second, when they do decide to halt a conflict, a multilateral organization can be an effective instrument for imposing such a joint decision. In the Lebanese case, the peacekeeping force that was agreed on at the same time was only a fig leaf for Syria and had no multilateral character.

Two multilateral organizations of a non-regional character intervened in the case of the Afghan invasion and in that of the Iran-Iraq war. They were the Islamic Conference Organization (ICO) and the nonaligned movement (NAM). Rubin describes the work of the ICO's Peace Committee in the Iran-Iraq war, unsuccessful though it has been to date, as a promising multilateral effort to settle the conflict. The ICO is an organization acceptable to Iran, although it too has been charged by the Iranians with not being sufficiently critical of Iraq. The NAM also put itself forward as a possible mediator in that war. The two organizations took up the Afghan invasion as well, passing resolutions condemning it and, in the case of the ICO, calling on members to consider boycotting the Olympic games in Moscow. The effect of these measures has been to reinforce the effort of the General Assembly to bring moral pressure to bear on the Soviet Union and to establish a set of principles for settling the conflict.

National States and Ad Hoc Groupings of States

National governments, acting unilaterally or in informal concert with other governments, have intervened with important consequences in two of the six conflicts: the Chadian and the Lebanese civil wars. The results have been very mixed, but on the whole these interventions have shown a greater capacity to affect the conflict than any of the multilateral efforts have demonstrated.

In Chad, the outside state most deeply involved has been France. The first three military interventions by the French were for the purpose of suppressing the conflict while Paris attempted to exact reforms from the Chadian government that would solve the underlying issues of the conflict. The reform efforts ultimately failed; the balance achieved between the warring parties by the French military presence was upset; and the fighting began again. A Libyan military intervention in 1980 had the same result. A later French intervention in 1983, to counter a Libyan invasion, was successful in achieving what Zartman terms a "hurting stalemate"—one that the contending parties find untenable and that threatens to lead to an even worse situation for both sides. Such a stalemate, he contends, is a prerequisite for conflict management and perhaps resolution. Taking advantage of this stalemate, the French undertook to mediate a political solution. Zartman draws from their experience, which was partly successful and could have been more so had they stuck it out, that a successful mediator must have legitimacy, a stake in the outcome, and, most important, leverage. A mediator need not be impartial, as is often thought necessary. Indeed, a mediator associated with one side may have the advantage of being able to deliver the agreement of that side, as the United States has often been expected to do with Israel in Middle East conflicts. In general, Zartman's argument points to the advantages of an engaged outside state over other possible mediators, provided the government of that state can deliver an outcome acceptable to both sides.

The Lebanese case provides an instructive counterpoint to the Chadian experience. Syria intervened with considerable force in 1976 primarily to create a stalemate and to mediate a settlement, as the French ultimately were able to do in Chad. Damascus found that stalemates in Lebanon were mercurial, however. There were so many players in the country, and so many external backers, that stalemates were quickly overturned.

Only once, in the fall of 1976, were the Syrians able to create a situation in which they could severely punish the two major contending forces, the Palestine Liberation Organization and the Maronite Christians, and in which outside governments were concerned enough to support a cease-fire. Even so, Syria found it impossible to produce a political outcome satisfactory to all the parties—there were many more than two—and the stalemate collapsed. The Syrians eventually became simply another contending force, a fate the French were not exposed to in Chad in the 1980's, in part because the strength of their military intervention was so much greater than that of the local parties.

Political interventions by the United States in the Lebanese conflict demonstrated the advantages, pointed to by Zartman, that are enjoyed by an intervening state that has a close association with one of the parties. The most important political efforts by Washington involved Israel and achieved what success they had largely by virtue of the confidence Israel has in the United States and the leverage the United States has, however limited, over Israel. The negotiation of the "red line" modus vivendi between Syrian invading forces and Israel in 1976 and the various cease-fires negotiated by Ambassador Philip Habib in 1981 and 1982 were cases in point.

Israel, of course, carried out major interventions in Lebanon, as well. In the main these were for the purpose of prosecuting the conflict with the PLO on Lebanese territory, and were not efforts to manage or to resolve the civil war. The 1982 Israeli invasion did have as one of its goals the establishment of a Lebanese government friendly to Israel, but Israel attempted to accomplish this through sheer force with no effort to resolve any of the underlying domestic political issues. Force inevitably proved insufficient, and the local faction that Israel had chosen as its proxy could not achieve legitimacy. The effort collapsed, showing as the French and Syrian experiences had shown that external force unaccompanied by resolution of the internal political dispute cannot provide a reliable and durable end to a civil conflict. This is especially true, as Zartman points out with respect to Chad, if other external powers remain free to support factions that do not accept the solution being imposed, as Syria was free to do in Lebanon in 1982–83.

Other efforts have been made by individual governments to moderate or to resolve these two conflicts as well as the Iran-Iraq war. As Zartman says about the African governments that sought separate roles in mediating the Chadian dispute, however, most were too weak to play more than "a purely facilitating or communicating version of a mediator's role." Since communication was not the principal problem in these disputes, such interventions were of little value. Harbeson speaks of action by regional states to contain and to disaggregate the Ethiopian-

Somalian dispute, but he is referring to policies pursued by neighboring states in managing their own relations with one or both of the parties. These states were not primarily attempting to influence the course of the dispute between Ethiopia and Somalia. The point Harbeson makes is, nonetheless, an important one. Concerted efforts to manage or to resolve a complex dispute could well approach the central problem by peeling away and dealing separately with other issues that make this problem complex and difficult when taken at one bite. As Harbeson also suggests, this is a delicate and ambiguous method for which multilateral organizations—especially the United Nations—seem to be ill-suited—though it is the strategy the world body employed with some initial successes in the Iran-Iraq war. Harbeson's observation suggests another conclusion as well, namely that in some cases the best treatment for disputes is provided by the normal, self-interested diplomatic activity of individual neighboring states.

Ad hoc groupings of states intervened in the Chadian and Lebanese wars but had little success. Efforts by Chad's neighbors in 1979 did produce a national unity government, but it was short-lived. A peace-keeping force agreed on by the same neighboring states was singularly ineffective; most of the national units composing the force never even arrived on the scene and the one that did shortly departed. In Lebanon, two informally organized peacekeeping forces—Multinational Force I (MNF I) and MNF II—were inserted by the United States, France, Italy, and, in the case of MNF II, Britain. MNF I had a limited mandate and a short life span, and it served its purpose adequately. MNF II found itself in a highly partisan role, however, caught in a continuing fight between powerful local factions. Without widely recognized legitimacy or a clear mandate (mandate from whom, in any case?), with differing interpretations of the mandate and differing operational methods among the national units, and with no overall command, it failed, suffering severe losses in the process.

The poor results in both conflicts suggest that ad hoc groupings have the disadvantages of both unilateral national operations and organized multilateral operations without the advantages of either. National in-terventions can be well-coordinated and single of purpose, and can bring to bear a great deal of power. They are frequently of questionable legitimacy, however, and are likely to become simply another party to the conflict. Multilateral forces—those of the United Nations—have legitimacy and competent leadership and organization. They are less likely to become caught up in the local conflict. On the other hand, they do not have the force or the unity of political purpose to bring about and enforce a stalemate, and thus are limited to a true peacekeeping role that can be successful only in certain conditions—a well-established cease-fire, commitment of the responsible parties to support the force, etc. Peacekeeping forces of regional organizations, if the OAU and Arab League forces in Chad and Lebanon were representative, have more the character of ad hoc groupings than of true multinational operations. And indeed they are in a sense ad hoc, since neither organization can provide effective staff or leadership for such a force, which must then rely on arrangements primarily among governments for the particular operation. The OAU requested assistance from the UN Security Council for its intervention in Chad, but the Council sat on the request for a long time and then turned it down. Council members do not want to be involved even to such an extent as that in an exercise over which they have no control or even influence. Moreover, this particular operation was doubtless seen as a bad investment, unlikely to succeed however much help the United Nations provided.

Summing Up

A number of conclusions are suggested by the six case studies and by the foregoing analysis that can help in thinking more profitably and realistically about the management and resolution of local conflicts. They are all subject to two caveats: that real-life disputes are sui generis, too complex and distinguished from one another by distinctions that are too subtle for any rigid guidelines to be applicable across the board; and that generalizations of enduring validity cannot be derived with assurance from a few cases covering a limited time span, although it is reasonable to assume that characteristics observed in these six quite different cases have significance beyond this sampling.

Complementary Operations

The first and most important conclusion is that each type of potential intervenor has somewhat different comparative advantages. They can be summarized very roughly as follows, recognizing that there are exceptions to every generality.

The United Nations—comprising the deliberative bodies and the Secretary General and his Secretariat staff—seems to enjoy the greatest comparative advantage in providing to an intervention legitimacy, impartiality, entrée to the parties, skill, experience, and an established organization and procedures. Regional organizations and non-global organizations other than those that are regional in character (e.g., the Islamic Conference Organization) generally share within their own spheres the legitimacy the United Nations enjoys globally, as well as entrée to the parties. They usually have less skill and experience, however, and seldom have the established organization and procedures for carrying operations beyond the deliberative stage. They have the advantages, on the other hand, that they can help isolate a dispute from the global system, especially the superpower competition, and that they can employ a looser and more informal style of diplomacy without the pressures of the United Nations.

The comparative advantage of individual states and ad hoc groups of states is quite different. They have dubious legitimacy in most, though not all, cases, and most of them have less experience, skill, or established organization and procedures for conflict management and resolution. But the larger states can frequently bring to bear far more pressure— political, military, or economic—to induce compliance by the parties. And they may also enjoy relationships of trust with one or more of the parties that give them special influence. Their comparative advantage, therefore, lies in persuasion, inducement, and enforcement.

The differing comparative advantages of the various potential inter- venors suggest that the most effective interventions may combine two or more actors in complementary efforts. One example was the successful effort in March 1978 to effect the withdrawal of Israeli forces from Lebanon. The United Nations contributed legitimacy and the peace- keeping force, and the United States provided influence with Israel. A somewhat different example, involving two parts of the United Nations, was the combination of UN Secretariat-sponsored fact-finding, a Security Council judgment based on it, and the Secretary General's appeal to the parties based in turn on the Council action—a combination that for a time at least seemed to prevent the use of chemical warfare in the Iran-Iraq war. US influence with Israel was usefully combined with UN access to the PLO in working out a cease-fire in Lebanon in 1981.

A logical combination, for example, would be fact-finding by the UN Secretariat, a fair judgment by the UN Security Council, and the use of adequate pressure—economic, political, or military—by member states to enforce it. It is the lack of this judgment-enforcement combination that, as much as anything else, has put the United Nations on the sidelines. In today's international climate, states are not likely to put their force behind UN decisions simply in order to give effect to them, however. But the same effect might be achieved in other ways. As a simplistic example, if one or more states are sufficiently concerned about a conflict to employ some degree of pressure to end it or to manage it, a coordinated parallel approach could include both UN actions— fact-finding, appeals by the Secretary General, conceivably a resolution by the Security Council (although this is more difficult to choreograph)— and over the same period a process of diplomatic contacts and graduated coercive measures by those states with enough interest in the situation to so involve themselves.

Another way to think about complementary efforts is to consider conflicts as latticeworks of separate but interlocking dimensions and phases. The Lebanese war is an exaggerated example, but illustrative. It began as a largely domestic struggle between religious, class, and clan groups, a struggle that persisted through all succeeding phases. With the entry into the fighting of large PLO forces, it took on a broader dimension, no longer entirely domestic; Syria's entry and later Israel's gave it a dominant regional cast; the PLO largely disappeared in 1982 and a totally new force—the Shiite Moslems—became key; and the process continues. During all these phases, several factors were present: problems of the political composition of succeeding governments; the political struggle over the constitutional power balance between Moslems and Christians; the maneuvering between factions in Lebanon and outside backers; outbursts of especially violent and deadly fighting with the dangers they posed for the civilian population; the kidnapping and assassination of foreigners as well as Lebanese; acts of terrorism— hijackings, bombings, etc; problems of refugees, civil order, hospital care, breakdown of supply systems, and a host of other crises.

The different phases and different compartments of a conflict can best be approached through different means as the international community attempts to isolate the war, to prevent the entry of new players, to contain and end the fighting, to reduce the loss of civilian life, to cope with terrorist incidents, and ultimately to resolve the basic issues. Some methods, some intervenors, may be more effective than others in dealing with particular parts of the problem. The best overall control effort is likely to be a mix of different forms of intervention by a variety of intervenors.

In especially long and complex conflicts it is frequently more useful to think in terms of managing or moderating particular aspects of it, as the UN Secretary General has tried to do in the Iran-Iraq war, rather than thinking of managing "the conflict" as a whole. Ideally, of course, in a serious and threatening dispute, a wide range of means, by a variety of intervenors, would be deployed to deal with many aspects simultaneously or sequentially, including efforts to resolve the conflict. In a variation of the point below about the relationship between managing and resolving, it can be difficult to make management of some aspects take hold without bringing other aspects under control at the same time.

Ideally, again, there should be some coordination of interventions undertaken by different actors. In practice, as our six examples illustrate, intervenors seldom have adequate control over the environment in which they act, or sufficient influence over the conflict, to plan refined strategies.

Nevertheless, the UN Secretary General is in a good position to keep in touch informally with concerned governments and regional or other organizations in order to coordinate their efforts or at least to keep them informed of what others plan.

This concept of complementary operations, or a mix of methods of dealing with a conflict, certainly offers no panacea. But it is a much more realistic direction to take in improving the capability of the international community to manage or to resolve disputes than the tinkering with UN mechanisms that is so often proposed. The means available to the Secretariat for fact-finding and keeping abreast of developments can usefully be improved, but more basic "reforms" such as upgrading the powers of the Security Council make little sense. The limitations under which the Council operates are not structural or mechanical, they are rooted in the attitudes of national governments and will continue to define the limits of the Council's effectiveness however the mechanism is changed.

Managing and Resolving:
The Relationship Between Them

The second point has to do with the relationship between managing and resolving disputes. Moderating a dispute through cease-fires and the like may prolong it. Escalation or the potential for it seems to be a prerequisite for resolving a dispute. But many disputes are so impervious to resolution that control may be the only recourse. On the other hand, control measures tend to collapse in time if no progress is made toward resolution. In theory, at least, states or organizations considering intervention in a dispute should attempt to assess how this relationship operates in the particular case. For a hurting stalemate to be created, for example, early steps to moderate the conflict could be counterproductive.

No Monopoly on Failure

A final, cautionary note. All the various means employed to control or to resolve the disputes in question failed more often than they succeeded. The United Nations, often criticized for its inability to prevent conflict, does not look so unsuccessful when its attempts are compared with efforts of national governments, for example. No means has a monopoly on failure, and all encounter the same bitter reality: conflicts within or between states spring from causes that are of vital importance to the participants and are singularly resistant to outside ministration.

Notes

1. It is useful to distinguish escalation, as used here, from intensification. Escalation refers to distinct, although not always easily perceived, steps—an upward ratcheting of the conflict. Intensification is a gradual increase in scope or violence, and occurs in almost all conflicts. For a fuller discussion see I. William Zartman, *Ripe for Resolution: Conflict and Intervention in Africa* (New York: Oxford University Press, 1985).

Index